Reformed Theology is a school of historic, orthodox, confessional Christianity in which the sovereignty of God, the authority of Scripture, God's grace in salvation, the necessity and significance of the church, and covenant theology are maintained and emphasized. Dr. Jonathan Master clearly, briefly, and helpfully discusses the nature and definition of Reformed theology in these pages, and thus helps students, pastors, and church members to think through its content and implications. This is a welcome introduction and reflection.

—**Ligon Duncan**, Chancellor and CEO, Reformed Theological Seminary

Pastors have long needed an introduction to the Reformed faith that is brief but comprehensive, deep but accessible, simple but compelling. Jonathan Master has provided us with such a resource in *Reformed Theology*, one that I suspect we will be handing out to interested people for years to come.

—**Terry L. Johnson**, Senior Minister, Independent Presbyterian Church, Savannah, Georgia

Jonathan Master provides an adept, warm, and engaging introduction to Reformed theology. He succinctly demonstrates that the Reformed faith is biblical Christianity. Whether you are a pastor or layperson, this is a resource you'll definitely want to get your hands on.

—**Jon D. Payne**, Senior Pastor, Christ Church Presbyterian, Charleston, South Carolina

It's not often that a book so effectively condenses great ideas into a slim volume. But Jonathan Master has done that with his excellent introduction to Reformed theology. With both erudition and warmth, Master zeroes in on the fundamentals of Reformed theology in a way that demonstrates both its biblical coherence and pastoral warmth. I will be happily commending this book to the members of the church I serve.

—**Todd Pruitt**, Lead Pastor, Covenant Presbyterian Church, Harrisonburg, Virginia

Dr. Jonathan Master, in this focused and accessible volume, concisely explains, amplifies, and clarifies the theology that was proclaimed and preserved in the providence of God through the travails of the Reformation. In so doing, he manifestly reveals that Reformed theology is merely, yet profoundly, the Holy Spirit empowered return to a theology revealed through the Bible, thereby liberating God's people from the superstitions and errors of ecclesiastically enforced theological heresies and reaffirming *sola Scriptura*—Scripture alone is our only rule of faith and practice.

—**Harry L. Reeder III**, Senior Pastor, Briarwood Presbyterian Church, Birmingham, Alabama

Jonathan Master's *Reformed Theology* is a joy to read. At once crystal clear and scripturally faithful, it covers the landscape theologically and practically without getting sidetracked in minutia or bogged down in complexity. Like the other volumes in this series, this new volume helps to address many of the questions people who are new to a Reformed church often have, but Master's volume in particular should awaken readers' appetites for still more of the riches of biblical doctrine well taught. This book made me freshly grateful for the soul-nourishing, intellectually satisfying, and worship-inspiring truths of Reformed theology, and for that I am deeply grateful.

—**David Strain**, Senior Pastor, First Presbyterian Church, Jackson, Mississippi

Jonathan Master is a thoughtful and gracious churchman, and this volume gives ample testimony to that. In brief compass, Dr. Master sets forth the basic principles of the Reformed faith, culminating, as all theology should, in doxology. For any who associate Reformed theology with dry intellectualism or self-righteous pedantry, this little volume will be a welcome corrective. Ideal for new Christians, small group discussion, and anyone wanting a brief account of why the Reformed faith is so important.

—**Carl R. Trueman**, Professor of Biblical and Religious Studies, Grove City College

REFORMED
THEOLOGY

BLESSINGS OF THE FAITH

A Series

Jason Helopoulos
Series Editor

Covenantal Baptism, by Jason Helopoulos
Expository Preaching, by David Strain
Persistent Prayer, by Guy M. Richard
Reformed Theology, by Jonathan Master

REFORMED
THEOLOGY

JONATHAN MASTER

PUBLISHING
P.O. BOX 817 • PHILLIPSBURG • NEW JERSEY 08865-0817

If you find this book helpful, consider writing a review online
—or contact P&R at editorial@prpbooks.com with your comments.
We'd love to hear from you.

Printed in the United States of America

Library of Congress Cataloging-in-Publication Data

Names: Master, Jonathan L., author.
Title: Reformed theology / Jonathan Master.
Description: Phillipsburg, New Jersey : P&R Publishing, [2023] | Series:
  Blessings of the faith | Summary: "What is Reformed theology? This short
  book serves as a helpful primer for church leaders, study groups, and
  individuals who want a well-rounded overview. Includes practical Q&A"--
  Provided by publisher.
Identifiers: LCCN 2022045289 | ISBN 9781629954097 (hardcover) | ISBN
  9781629954547 (epub)
Subjects: LCSH: Reformed Church--Doctrines.
Classification: LCC BX9422.3 .M27 2023 | DDC 230/.42--dc23/eng/20230110
LC record available at https://lccn.loc.gov/2022045289

To my father and mother,
John Reis Master
and
Janet Crawford Master

CONTENTS

FOREWORD

It has often been said—sometimes with a sense of humor and sometimes in annoyance—that Presbyterian and Reformed churches love to do things "decently and in order." I can understand both the humor and the frustration that lie behind that sentiment. We love our plans, our minutes, our courts, and our committees. Presbyterian and Reformed folks have been known to appoint committees just to oversee other committees (reminding me of the old *Onion* headline that announced "New Starbucks Opens in Rest Room of Existing Starbucks"). We like doing things so decently that we expect our church officers to know three things: the Bible, our confessions, and a book with *Order* in its title.

But before we shake our heads in disbelief at those uber-Reformed types (physician, heal thyself!), we should recall that before "decently and in order" was a Presbyterian predilection, it was a biblical command (see 1 Cor. 14:40). Paul's injunction for the church to be marked by propriety and decorum, to be well-ordered like troops drawn up in ranks, is a fitting conclusion to a portion of Scripture that deals with confusion regarding gender, confusion at the Lord's Table, confusion about spiritual gifts, confusion in the body of Christ, and confusion in public worship. "Decently and in order" sounds pretty good compared to the mess that prevailed in Corinth.

A typical knock on Presbyterian and Reformed Christians is that though supreme in head, they are deficient in heart. We are the emotionless stoics, the changeless wonders, God's frozen chosen. But such veiled insults would not have impressed the apostle Paul, for he knew that the opposite of order in the church is not free-flowing spontaneity; it is self-exalting chaos. God never favors confusion over peace (see 1 Cor. 14:33). He never pits theology against doxology or head against heart. David Garland put it memorably: "The Spirit of ardor is also the Spirit of order."[1]

When Jason Helopoulos approached me about writing a foreword for this series, I was happy to oblige—not only because Jason is one of my best friends (and we both root for the hapless Chicago Bears) but because these careful, balanced, and well-reasoned volumes will occupy an important place on the book stalls of Presbyterian and Reformed churches. We need short, accessible books written by thoughtful, seasoned pastors for regular members on the foundational elements of church life and ministry. That's what we need, and that's what this series delivers: wise answers to many of the church's most practical and pressing questions.

This series of books on Presbyterian and Reformed theology, worship, and polity is not a multivolume exploration of 1 Corinthians 14:40, but I am glad it is unapologetically written with Paul's command in mind. The reality is that every church will worship in some way, pray in some way, be led in some way, be structured in some way, and do baptism and the Lord's Supper in some way. Every church is living out some form of theology—even if that theology is based on pragmatism instead of biblical principles. Why wouldn't we want the life we share in the church to be shaped by the best exegetical, theological, and historical reflections? Why wouldn't we want to be thoughtful instead of thoughtless? Why wouldn't we want all things in the life we live together to be done decently and in good order? That's not the Presbyterian and Reformed way. That's God's way, and Presbyterian and Reformed Christians would do well not to forget it.

Kevin DeYoung
Senior Pastor, Christ Covenant Church
Matthews, North Carolina

Introduction

THEOLOGY MATTERS

This book arises out of two simple convictions. The first is that knowing what we believe about God, humanity, worship, and salvation is important. More than important, it is vital. We need clear answers to the biggest questions in life and the most consequential matters of eternity. These answers must be true—everything depends on it.

Knowing these true answers and being able to articulate them is a powerful thing. Not only must we be clear and thoughtful about what we believe, but we ought to be able to present our beliefs with a coherence that displays their inner logic. The pieces should fit together. This kind of clarity and coherence brings stability to our lives, to our families, and to our witness in the world.

If you are a new Christian, it is important for you to gain a foothold in the teaching of the whole Bible and to have ready answers for the biggest and most fundamental theological questions. If you have been a Christian for some time, you need to know where you stand and to orient your worship, fellowship, and practice in a way that accords with your convictions. Having a basic theological framework is essential. And this is the first conviction on which this book is based: theological frameworks matter.

The second conviction follows directly from the first: Reformed theology is a blessing. It may sound strange to call a theological system a blessing. If you have preconceived notions about Reformed theology, it may sound especially odd. But, strange or not, this book is written with the conviction that it is true.

A caricature suggests that theology is only for those who have special training or a vocation to serve as Christian ministers. Sometimes it seems as if the people who are most interested in debating theological nuances are socially awkward and unable to connect with regular people and their typical questions about life. If this has been your experience or your impression, please understand that this book is still for you. Reformed theology, rightly understood, cuts through a false association between theological thinking and ivory-tower speculation. One of the great early Reformed theologians defined theology simply as "the doctrine of living to God through Christ."[1] It is a theology for living to God. It is about life.

So if you are looking for answers to the biggest questions about life and eternity, then the Christian faith—and the Reformed expression of that faith—provides them. Not only are the answers coherent, logical, and clear, they are true. They are all centered on the person and work of the Lord Jesus Christ. They are truths found in him and discovered through his Word, the Bible.

Reformed theology, centered on Jesus Christ and rooted in the Scriptures, seeks to explain the whole Bible by showing God's work of salvation from beginning to end. It gives an honest assessment of humanity and good news about the nature of salvation. More than that, it shows how the Bible instructs us personally, teaching us how we should worship God and serve him in our everyday lives at home, at work, and in the church. Truth is always a blessing, but these truths give special life and clarity.

In order to introduce these things, we must first spend some time on definitions. The first chapter will be devoted to answering the question "What is Reformed theology?" After this, we can spend the next two chapters looking more closely at the Bible to see how all these truths are expressed and how they unfold. Next we will examine the blessings that come to us from this expression of biblical truth. Finally, following the format of this series, we will answer a series of questions about Reformed theology.

Theology matters. Understanding and explaining it with clarity is vital. And the expression of biblical truth will affect the whole of our lives. When God's truth transforms our thinking, the blessings go beyond any expectation.

1

WHAT IS REFORMED THEOLOGY?

What is Reformed theology? What does it mean if your church is referred to as *Reformed* or if a presentation of the Bible's teaching is Reformed? People in Reformed congregations ask one another, "When did you become Reformed?" or "What made you look for a Reformed church?" Maybe such questions have been addressed to you.

But what do these questions mean? What are they driving at? Are they important? And if so, how are you to understand and answer them?

Answering these common questions can be surprisingly complex. This is partly because the word *Reformed* has a long history and has been used in many different ways. Sometimes *Reformed theology* is used in a strictly historical sense and sometimes in a more theological sense. Sometimes it is meant to be precise and technical, but often its meaning is fairly basic.

Historical and Popular Views

At its most basic level, the term *Reformed theology* refers to the theological conclusions that flowed out of the Protestant Reformation. The early Reformers—such as Martin Luther, Ulrich Zwingli, and John Calvin—had sharp and specific criticisms of Roman Catholic theology as it had developed in the Middle Ages. Among other things, the Reformers believed that Roman Catholic worship was unbiblical; they rejected the Roman Catholic teaching on the nature of justification and the place of individual saving faith. They also rejected Roman Catholic claims about the authority of the pope, asserting that the Bible alone held the place of final authority in discussions of doctrine. They taught that salvation comes through God's grace alone, by faith alone. They rejected the Roman Catholic understanding of the place and meaning of baptism and communion, returning to the biblical definition of these important sacraments of Christ. These were historical concerns, but they still lie at the heart of what it means to be Reformed.

Within this general Protestant framework, there were divisions. Luther and those who followed him had different approaches from Calvin and the other European Reformers. These differences—largely on the sacraments and worship—set Lutherans apart from the other Protestants. Those who followed Luther became known as *Lutherans*; those who followed the other Reformers are generally referred to as *Reformed*.

So, from a historical perspective, *Reformed theology* refers to the theology of the non-Lutheran teaching that flows out of the Protestant Reformation. When the term is used in this historical way (as in much scholarly literature), it also normally implies adherence to one of the historical confessions of faith that bind together Reformed congregations and denominations.

In popular usage, Reformed theology is often identified with the so-called "five points of Calvinism":

1. *Total depravity:* the belief that human beings are corrupt at their core because of the sin of Adam.
2. *Unconditional election:* the belief that God chooses those whom he saves out of his own sovereign love, not out of anything the recipients of that love have in themselves.
3. *Limited atonement:* the belief that Christ's death pays the ransom for a particular people and his salvation is definite.
4. *Irresistible grace:* the belief that God's grace accomplishes its intended result in those who are saved.
5. *Perseverance of the saints:* the belief that those who are saved by God in Christ will be preserved to the end.

All of these beliefs are indeed important teachings of the Reformed tradition. Although they were not specifically organized according to the acronym by which they are known today (TULIP) until centuries later, they arose as a response to false teachers who had infiltrated the Reformed community in the early 1600s. Nonetheless, as helpful as these five points are in summarizing key biblical truths about salvation, they do not fully encapsulate, or accurately describe, all of Reformed theology.

Today when people in evangelical churches refer to "Reformed theology" or to "being Reformed," they often mean something less historically grounded. It is often the case today that when someone refers to holding to "Reformed theology," they mean that they believe that God's sovereign grace is at work in electing and saving sinners (the doctrine of predestination) and that God's Word is inspired and inerrant and has absolute authority.

The Five *Solas* of the Reformation

There are better ways to define the term *Reformed theology*, however. For John Calvin and other early reformers, the Reformation was not just about the doctrine of salvation. Worship was of central significance as well. Beyond these two primary concerns, there were other matters of faith and practice inextricably linked with Reformed teaching. Because of this, many have suggested a more full-orbed starting place in defining Reformed theology known as the "five *solas* of the Reformation." The five *solas* (*sola* is the Latin word for "only" or "alone") are *sola Scriptura* (Scripture alone); *sola fide* (faith alone); *sola gratia* (grace alone);

solus Christus (Christ alone); and *soli Deo gloria* (God's glory alone). Put together, these five affirmations express very clearly the central concerns of the Protestant Reformation.

Sola Scriptura

Reformed Christians emphasize that Scripture alone (*sola Scriptura*) is the final authority in our faith and practice. At the time of the Protestant Reformation, the late-medieval Roman Catholic church maintained that Scripture, although inspired and without error, was to be interpreted on the basis of other forms of authority, namely church tradition and the official proclamations of the pope. Effectively this meant that church tradition and papal teaching were greater authorities, since interpretations of the Bible were always subject to them.

This approach had profound consequences for what could be taught in the church and led to a church in which, functionally speaking, the Bible was not given much direct attention at all. Regular Christians were denied access to the Bible in their own language and were instead commanded to blindly obey church teaching. Even those members of the priesthood who were allowed to study the Bible were closely monitored so that their teaching did not threaten the current practices of the Roman Catholic church. In large part, this is what led to Martin Luther's excommunication.

The earliest Reformers argued that the Roman Catholic approach to the Bible was a gross error. Fundamentally, it denied the basic nature of Scripture as God's Word. The Bible is inspired by God, without error, and fundamentally authoritative.[1] To undermine these truths is to turn against God's revealed Word. The Reformers also argued that the Roman Catholic approach to Scripture was a distortion of what the church had always believed. Tradition was on the Reformers' side, and the late-medieval church had moved away from what the apostles and the earliest leaders in the church believed and taught.

Today, the principle of *sola Scriptura* means our theology and our worship must always be based on the Bible. The Scriptures alone are the final arbiter and guide for faith and practice. We do not live in the world of the late Middle Ages, so our temptation to substitute the Bible's authority may not come from the pope or from church tradition. More often, it comes from the teaching of those in our culture—from sociologists, scientists, politicians, and entertainers—who sometimes seek to stand in authority over the Bible. When popular cultural teaching is the final authority, churches and individual Christians may believe only those things in the Bible that do not conflict with the authority of cultural elites.

This is especially important when it comes to the question of worship, which, as we have seen, was of central importance in the Reformation. How are we to approach God? When are we to do so and in what manner? How can we know what he finds acceptable? Reformed theology teaches that God has answered all these questions in the Bible. Scripture alone is the guide to our worship, and any practice that goes beyond the teaching of the scripture must be rejected.

Some within the church place their own feelings and experiences above the Word of God. This was happening in the time of the Reformation as well. Those who do this follow the Bible unless it conflicts with their wishes, experiences, or private inclinations. Sometimes the emotions and inclinations are deeply felt; sometimes they involve claims about supernatural revelation or personal encounters with God. In every case, pressure is applied to submit God's Word to an individual feeling or experience as the final authority.

Whatever the competing authority—the pope, the cultural elite, or a private feeling—the Reformed doctrine of *sola Scriptura* asserts that the Bible alone must have the final word. It is God's uniquely inspired testimony, and Christians throughout history have recognized that it alone is the authority for our teaching, our ethical decisions, and our practice of worship.

Sola Fide

Reformed theology teaches that human beings are separated from God by nature. The Bible is clear about this. For example, the apostle Paul writes the following to the Ephesian church:

> You were dead in the trespasses and sins in which you once walked, following the course of this world, following the prince of the power of the air, the spirit that is now

at work in the sons of disobedience—among whom we
all once lived in the passions of our flesh, carrying out
the desires of the body and the mind, and were by nature
children of wrath, like the rest of mankind. (Eph. 2:1–3)

These are strong words. Elsewhere, Paul writes that all
human beings "exchanged the truth about God for a lie
and worshipped and served the creature rather than the
Creator, who is blessed forever" (Rom. 1:25). The Old Testament prophet Jeremiah has an equally harsh assessment
of our situation: "The heart is deceitful above all things,
and desperately sick" (Jer. 17:9).

Because the human condition is so bleak, the Bible also
teaches that there is nothing that people can do—no works
they can perform or good deeds they can practice—that
can win them favor with God. It is by *faith alone* that we
can be saved. The apostle Paul writes,

All have sinned and fall short of the glory of God, and
are justified by his grace as a gift, through the redemption that is in Christ Jesus, whom God put forward as
a propitiation by his blood, *to be received by faith* . . . so
that he might be just and the justifier of *the one who has
faith* in Jesus. (Rom. 3:23–26)

In the same passage in which Paul describes human beings
as children of wrath by nature, he goes on to say, "By grace
you have been saved through faith" (Eph. 2:8).

This truth that sinners can be justified only through faith was so important to the Reformers that it was called the "material cause" of the Protestant Reformation. By this, the Reformers meant that justification by faith alone is the matter out of which the Reformation was made. It is still a point of contention between Protestants and Roman Catholics and remains a key feature of Reformed theology.

When we assert that salvation is through faith alone, we mean that faith is the instrument by which we grasp God's promises in Christ. We do not lay claim to Christ savingly through our works, our baptism, our church membership, or our ethnic identity. Yet real faith will and must lead to good works. The change that takes place in a Christian is so profound that he or she should be recognizable by the fruit of the Spirit. Christians should put sin to death and form new habits, but they grasp the promises of salvation in Christ through faith alone.

Sola Gratia

Because *sola fide* (faith alone) played such a key role in the Protestant Reformation, it is mentioned just after *sola Scriptura* in our summary of Reformed theology. But there is a strong sense in which *sola fide* can be understood only in light of *sola gratia* (grace alone). This is because the major Bible passages that teach that salvation comes through faith alone also emphasize that it is God's grace alone that saves us.

Consider Ephesians 2:8, for instance. This verse makes it clear that salvation is received through faith.

But this acknowledgment is surrounded by reminders that all salvation comes by God's grace. "*For by grace you have been saved through faith. And this is not your own doing; it is the gift of God*" (Eph. 2:8). Salvation comes through faith, but even that faith is a gift from God. All salvation is by grace.

This is underscored when we remember our natural status as sinners. None of us can earn a place in God's favor. We could never be justified by works. And because we are helpless before God, everything we receive from him is a gift. It is grace alone.

This is the place for us also to examine the doctrine of predestination, which many rightly associate with Reformed theology. Reformed theologians emphasize God's election because it is biblical (*sola Scriptura*), but also because it so clearly shows that all salvation is a work of God (*sola gratia*). It simply refers to the biblical truth that God chooses those whom he saves.

In Ephesians 1, Paul writes, "In love [God] *predestined* us for adoption to himself as sons through Jesus Christ, according to the purpose of his will, to the praise of his glorious grace" (vv. 4–6). In Romans 9, Paul writes about "God's purpose of election," which "continue[s], not because of works, but because of him who calls" (v. 11). In other words, the teaching of election reveals with unique clarity that Christians do not save themselves. God chose us, so that his glory would be displayed and his grace would be magnified in our salvation.

This should lead us to further praise of God and confidence in him. Since salvation is his work, he will complete it. Since it is dependent on grace and not on our feeble efforts, we can be assured that God will finish the task he has begun (see Phil. 1:6).

Solus Christus

The Protestant Reformers and the Roman Catholic church agreed on the nature of Christ. They affirmed that Jesus Christ is the incarnate Son of God, truly divine and truly human, one Person with two natures (divine and human) that are united together. Christ is to be worshiped and served. Neither the Reformers nor the Catholics disputed that the incarnate Christ was born of a virgin, crucified on a cross, and raised from the dead before he ascended into heaven. Where Luther and the other Reformers disagreed with the late-medieval Roman church was on how Christ reigns, how he communicates his benefits to his church, how he is to be worshiped, and how completely his death satisfies God's justice with respect to individual sinners.

As with all the *solas* we have examined, the *alone* here is vitally important. The Roman Catholic church did not deny the importance or centrality of Jesus Christ. In their practice, however, they did deny the final, once-for-all nature of Christ's atoning sacrifice. They taught, and continue to teach, that in the mass Christ is offered for the propitiation of sins in an "unbloody manner."[2] The Roman church also taught that the benefits of Christ's grace are conferred through the sacraments and that Christ's body and blood are physically present in the mass. This not only struck at the gracious nature of salvation to be received by faith alone but also compromised the reality of Christ's physical bodily presence in heaven.

The principle of *solus Christus* also relates to the question of authority. Is Christ *alone* the head of the church, mediating his authority through his Word, or is there a representative of Christ on earth—another mediator between God and man? Furthermore, is God through Christ alone the one to whom we pray, or are Mary and other dead Christians additional mediators between us and God?

Once the principle of Christ alone is established, it transforms the way the Bible is understood and preached. The apostle Paul wrote, "I decided to know nothing among you except Jesus Christ and him crucified" (1 Cor. 2:2). The proclamation of Christ alone in preaching—as the object of faith, the ruler of the church, the risen and ascended God-man—was and continues to be a unifying principle of Reformed theology.

Soli Deo Gloria

The last of the five *solas* is the natural outworking of the first four. Reformed theology states that all of life is to be understood in terms of the glory of God. To be Reformed in our thinking is to be God-centered. We recognize that our salvation is from the Lord and that even our existence is a gift from him. To ascribe our salvation to anyone else or to worship anything or anyone else is to rob God of the glory due his name.

The Bible reminds us that "in [God] we live and move and have our being" (Acts 17:28). We are taught that Christ "upholds the universe by the word of his power" (Heb. 1:3). It follows from this that our guiding principle ought to be "whether you eat or drink, or whatever you do, do all to the glory of God" (1 Cor. 10:31).

The Covenant

Beyond the five *solas*, Reformed theology has always been closely identified with *covenant theology*. In the Scriptures, God works out his saving purposes by means of successive covenants. As we will see, a covenant is an agreement between two parties with duties, promises, and obligations. In fact, the Bible speaks of an overarching "eternal covenant" (Heb. 13:20) that centers on the cross of Christ. Covenants provide the biblical framework by which we understand God's work in Christ and his dealings with his people throughout history.

The centrality of the covenantal structure in the Bible and the Christian life can hardly be overstated, and the ramifications of this central theme in the Scriptures are significant. Indeed, this is one of the reasons that merely emphasizing predestination, or even the five points of Calvinism, does not do justice to what it means to be a

Reformed Christian. Reformed theology is whole-Bible theology, and the covenant is the biblical framework that shows the unity of both the Old Testament and the New.

The Confessions

Lastly, all vibrant and enduring Reformed traditions have confessions of faith that give written expression to their convictions. The best-known of the mature Reformed confessions include the Belgic Confession, the Heidelberg Catechism, and the Canons of Dort (which together are called the Three Forms of Unity) and the Westminster Confession of Faith, which has its own catechisms.

From the earliest days, Reformed Christians assumed that Reformed theology would be expressed in confessions of faith. Therefore, to be Reformed is to be confessional; to be part of a Reformed church is to be in a place in which one of these historic confessions is professed, taught, and followed. We will look at this more closely in chapter 4.

Defining the terms *Reformed* and *Reformed theology* is not a simple task. But for our purposes, we might say that Reformed theology is a theology that (1) affirms the five *solas* and all their implications, (2) recognizes the centrality of the covenant in God's saving purposes, and (3) is expressed in a historic and public confession of faith.

With that in mind, we can move on to examine the teaching of the Bible on these points and to see how the truths treasured by the Reformers are a great blessing to God's people.

Questions for Further Reflection

1. Why is it important for us to understand terms like *Reformed theology*? How and where have you heard these terms used?
2. What makes the five *solas* a helpful summary of biblical teaching regarding salvation? Do they omit anything significant? What biblical questions do they raise?
3. Why are creeds and confessions necessary for the health of the church? In what ways do they protect us?

2

SCRIPTURE AND GOD'S SOVEREIGNTY

In the previous chapter, we explored the question of how to define Reformed theology, but now we must turn to the question of veracity. Is Reformed theology as we have defined it true?

The answer to this question must be found in the Bible itself. If the Bible doesn't point to the beliefs we identified in the last chapter, then they cannot qualify as core convictions from which we should draw our theological identity. (Remember, one of those core convictions is that Scripture alone is our final arbiter!) But if we find that they *are* in the Bible—and if they are central to the biblical witness to how we should engage in theological discussion and debate—then we must hold to them. More than that, we must rejoice in them.

In this chapter, we'll see that even the first few chapters of Scripture contain the seeds of Reformed theology. We'll also explore what Scripture has to say about God's sovereignty and its implications. But first we must answer a very important question.

Why Does the Bible Matter So Much?

One of the most consequential questions each of us must answer relates to the source of our authority. How can we arrive at a true knowledge of God? What guides our life decisions and our notions about reality? Where do we go to find definitive answers to moral questions?

The Scriptures are clear that they alone provide this kind of authority. David, writing about the Word of God, says this:

> The law of the LORD is perfect,
>   reviving the soul;
> the testimony of the LORD is sure,
>   making wise the simple;
> the precepts of the LORD are right,
>   rejoicing the heart;
> the commandment of the LORD is pure,
>   enlightening the eyes. (Ps. 19:7–8)

Many other psalms repeat this kind of language. Furthermore, in the New Testament, the apostle Paul writes, "All Scripture is breathed out by God and profitable for teaching, for reproof, for correction, and for training in righteousness" (2 Tim. 3:16). The Bible is clear about its own authority, sufficiency, and usefulness.

But perhaps this appears to be a circular argument. After all, just because the Bible claims that it has authority does not mean that it deserves to be held in such high esteem.

At this point, we could look at the ways in which the Bible proves its veracity in the form of historical accuracy, fulfilled prophecy, internal coherence, and power to change lives. But for Christians, there is also the witness of Jesus Christ. Again and again, Jesus made it clear that he held the Bible in the highest possible esteem. It was Jesus Christ, after all, who said in his most famous sermon,

> Do not think that I have come to abolish the Law or the Prophets; I have not come to abolish them but to fulfill them. For truly, I say to you, until heaven and earth pass away, not an iota, not a dot, will pass from the Law until all is accomplished. Therefore whoever relaxes one of the least of these commandments and teaches others to do the same will be called least in the kingdom of heaven, but whoever does them and teaches them will be called great in the kingdom of heaven. (Matt. 5:17–19)

The message of the remainder of his ministry was no different. Jesus taught that Scripture is accurate to its smallest details. He viewed it as historically accurate with respect to Adam and Eve (see Matt. 19:3–4), the flood (see Luke 17:26–27), and the account of Jonah (see Matt. 12:40). In one of his most sophisticated arguments, Jesus hinged his interpretation on the tense of a Hebrew verb in the Old Testament (see Matt. 22:32). Near the end of his life, when his disciples failed to understand his coming death and its implications, Jesus pointed them to the Scriptures: "Have you never read in the Scriptures: 'The stone that the builders rejected has become the cornerstone'?" (Matt. 21:42).

Even during his moment of greatest suffering, when Jesus was on the cross, the words of Scripture were on his lips. His actions, even under duress, all served to fulfill those same Scriptures. Even in his death, Jesus declared by his actions: Scripture cannot be broken.

After his death and resurrection, it was on this very point that Jesus rebuked some of his close followers:

> And he said to them, "O foolish ones, and slow of heart to believe all that the prophets have spoken! . . ." And beginning with Moses and all the Prophets, he interpreted to them in all the Scriptures the things concerning himself. (Luke 24:25, 27)

All this is to say that to be Christians—to truly trust in Jesus Christ and to follow him—we must hold to the traditional Christian teaching about the Bible. Scripture must be our final authority—our final court of appeal—precisely because we serve Christ. Along these lines, it is especially notable that the Bible is several times referred to as "the word of Christ" (Rom. 10:17; Col. 3:16). By following the Bible, we obey Christ. If we put anything in its place of authority—be it tradition, contemporary elite opinion, or our own individual preferences—we dishonor Jesus Christ and leave the path to which his followers must be committed.

We must, therefore, evaluate the beliefs we discussed in the previous chapter on the basis of the Bible to see if they are true. In so doing, we will examine whether or not they are central to our understanding of salvation by grace alone through faith alone in Christ alone to the glory of God alone.

Gleanings from Genesis

The book of Genesis, especially its first few chapters, contains most of the basic elements we outlined in chapter 1. Of course, we have a lot more than Genesis, and some of the truths we outlined are discussed in far more detail later in the Scriptures. But because the Bible is our authority, we will begin where the Bible begins.

The Bible starts with creation. Genesis opens with an account of how God made the heavens and the earth. This culminates in his creation of man and woman in his image and in God's own rest on the seventh day. This is followed by a more detailed description of the manner in which God made human beings and the initial environment in which he placed them.

These details about creation may seem mundane initially, or we may read them with a preoccupation about questions regarding the modern scientific theory of evolution. These questions are very important to strike head-on since they relate to the veracity of God's Word, but they are beyond the scope of this short study. Instead, we should note immediately that God alone is the Creator of all things. God is in charge from the beginning, and his word is used as the instrument to give life and to govern human existence.

This is no small matter, and it touches directly on some of the *solas* we explored in the last chapter. In Genesis 1, when God creates the heavens and the earth, he does so by his word. The phrase that is repeated over and over is "And God said." God's spoken declarations bring into existence the very thing he decrees. God's word is true, and it is powerful.

By Genesis 2, when God gives his commands to Adam, the authority of his word has already been established. In a sense, the Lord gives Adam a little Bible when he says, "You may surely eat of every tree of the garden, but of the tree of the knowledge of good and evil you shall not eat, for in the day that you eat of it you shall surely die" (Gen. 2:16–17). Adam's covenantal responsibility is clear. He is to be governed by the authority of the word of God—that same powerful, life-giving word that was the instrument of God's creation of him and of all things. God's word alone had this authority over Adam and over all who followed after him.

When Adam sins in the garden by disobeying God's command, disaster ensues, just as God warned it would.

Almost every verse in Genesis 3 records the world-changing effects of Adam and Eve's sin. Sin changes everything, both within their own hearts and among their surroundings.

Immediately after eating the forbidden fruit, Adam and Eve feel great shame over their nakedness, shame they never experienced before they sinned (see Gen. 3:7). In response to that shame, they seek to cover themselves. Worse still, they immediately try to hide from God, even though God is their Creator and has given them abundant blessings (see Gen. 3:8). Their entire posture toward God has changed. They now see him as an enemy and his presence as something to be avoided.

Their posture toward each other changes as well. At the end of Genesis 2, Adam spoke of Eve with love and gratitude: "This is now bone of my bones and flesh of my flesh" (v. 23). But after the fall, his attitude shifts, and he blames Eve for the entrance of sin into the world: "The woman whom you [God] gave to be with me, she gave me fruit of the tree, and I ate" (Gen. 3:12). Adam's blame-shifting shows his unwillingness to confess his sin and repent before God. But the fact that he blames his wife is also striking. Far from expressing the loving gratitude he voiced earlier, Adam looks on Eve as a curse from God and the source of his problems.

This pattern continues with Adam's descendants. Cain, his firstborn, is a murderer who rejects God. Those who follow Cain are worse still. Within a few chapters, we read that "the LORD saw that the wickedness of man was great in the earth, and that every intention of the thoughts of his heart was only evil continually" (Gen. 6:5). There could hardly be a more comprehensive statement of human depravity. It is an internal problem that increases from one generation to the next.

The record of the fall of man and its immediate consequences makes for difficult reading. But even while delivering the true and necessary bad news about us, the Bible also gives us remarkably good news. After the rebellion of Adam and Eve, the Lord curses the serpent who deceived Eve and tempted Adam to sin. He tells Satan, "I will put enmity between you and the woman, and between your offspring and her offspring; he shall bruise your head, and you shall bruise his heel" (Gen. 3:15).

As the book of Genesis continues, we see the remarkable significance of these words. God promised to raise up an offspring or "seed" who would destroy the serpent. The one who had opposed God's word would be struck down by One who would be an offspring of the woman. Theologians sometimes refer to this promise as the first gospel, because in it we see—in the earliest chapters of Genesis—God's good news about his coming Messiah who would deal the death blow to sin and Satan.

What we see in the first chapters of Genesis provides the initial outline of Reformed theology. Not all the elements appear in clear detail, but the template is clear: God is the sovereign Creator, in charge of all things; his Word is the rule of faith and practice; man is a fallen sinner, unable and unwilling to please God and incapable of saving himself; God, in his grace, will carry out his promised rescue of his people through a human Mediator who alone is suited to the task of defeating sin and Satan and accomplishing salvation.

God's Sovereignty over All

As we've seen, the simple fact that God is the Creator of all things makes his sovereignty clear. In fact, the apostle Paul indicates that since the creation, God's invisible attributes are on display and visible. He writes, "What can be known about God is plain to [people], because God has shown it to them. For his invisible attributes, namely, his eternal power and divine nature, have been clearly perceived, ever since the creation of the world, in the things that have been made" (Rom. 1:19–20). Creation shows that God alone is in charge; he alone has the right to demand obedience and allegiance. God's promise of salvation demonstrates that God is in charge of the future as well as the present and past. He can promise that something will take place, and the fulfillment of that promise is guaranteed.

This truth is both declared and displayed in many passages of Scripture. For example, in Ephesians 1, Paul refers to the work of God in salvation and places it within the framework of God's total sovereignty, writing that it is "according to the purpose of him who works all things according to the counsel of his will" (Eph. 1:11). God declares through the prophet Isaiah, "I am God, and there is none like me, declaring the end from the beginning and from ancient times things not yet done, saying, 'My counsel shall stand, and I will accomplish all my purpose'" (Isa. 46:9–10). Nebuchadnezzar, one of the great leaders of the ancient world, summarized God's sovereignty well: "He does according to his will among the host of heaven and among the inhabitants of the earth; and none can stay his hand or say to him, 'What have you done?'" (Dan. 4:35).

This truth about God's sovereignty is foundational to the system of Reformed theology. His sovereignty extends not only to the cosmic realities of creation but to the personal and seemingly private actions of individual people (see Ps. 139; Prov. 19:21). God is sovereign over everything.

The Necessity of God's Sovereignty for Our Salvation

As we have seen, human beings are oriented to run away from God. Though God's sovereignty is clearly seen in creation, the Bible teaches that people "by their unrighteousness suppress the truth" (Rom. 1:18). Man in his natural state is not able to overcome his basic inclination to sin, nor is he able to turn to God apart from divine intervention. Even God's Word seems like foolishness to him: "The natural person does not accept the things of the

Spirit of God, for they are folly to him, and he is not able to understand them because they are spiritually discerned" (1 Cor. 2:14). Elsewhere Paul writes, "The mind that is set on the flesh is hostile to God, for it does not submit to God's law; indeed, it cannot. Those who are in the flesh cannot please God" (Rom. 8:7–8).

This is why Reformed Christians place so much emphasis on the sovereignty of God over all things. The Bible teaches that if God is not sovereign over our lives—if, for instance, we are in control of all the things that we say or do—then we have no hope of ever being saved. As Jesus teaches his disciples, "Apart from me you can do nothing" (John 15:5).

The notion of the sovereignty of God is controversial in some circles. Some of this is natural. As we have seen, man in his natural state suppresses the truth about God's power, and it is often easier for us to look at our lives as testimonies to our ingenuity or expertise. Even many who read the Bible and claim a knowledge of God see the story of their salvation as one in which their decisions, desires, and deductions have played a central role. But, as we have seen, this is a profound misunderstanding—both of our own nature (fallen and sinful) and of who God is (Creator and sovereign). When it comes to our salvation, the Bible teaches that God deserves all the glory. Not only did he, through the death of his Son, provide the atoning sacrifice for sin, but he also, by means of election, sovereignly granted mercy to sinners who had rebelled against him.

The Doctrine of Election

The doctrine of election teaches that God chooses those individuals who will be saved. When many people think of the distinctives of Reformed theology, their minds immediately jump to this doctrine. Some mistakenly attribute its origin to John Calvin. Some argue that the doctrine of election is the key dividing line between those who identify their theology as Reformed and those who do not, and they attach the label *Reformed* to anyone who teaches divine election. Although we have seen that Reformed theology is much more than this, the fact remains that election does play a central role. Like so many important truths about salvation, election is introduced first in Genesis and then developed with even greater clarity later in Scripture.

As we have seen, the book of Genesis makes it clear that God is the sovereign Creator and that all humanity is fallen: bent away from God and guilty. This guilt and sin grows more pronounced as Genesis unfolds, though the promise God made to provide an offspring for the redemption of his people remains.

In Genesis 12, God's promise becomes more concrete as God chooses a man whom he calls Abraham and makes significant covenant promises to him. As we know, Abraham is integral to God's plan for the world. But what is considered less often is that Abraham was, like all people, naturally turned away from God. When God speaks later to the nation of Israel about his promises to Abraham, he does not glorify Abraham or highlight any inherent goodness in him. Instead, he emphasizes the fact that Abraham was an idolater in a faraway land: "Long ago, your fathers lived beyond the Euphrates, Terah, the father of Abraham and of Nahor; and they served other gods. Then I took your father Abraham" (Josh. 24:2–3). When God saved Abraham, it was God's choice. God elected Abraham to receive salvation.

The same is true of God's work among the nation of Israel. In Deuteronomy, election is in view when Moses tells the people,

> The LORD your God has chosen you to be a people for his treasured possession, out of all the peoples who are on the face of the earth. It was not because you were more in number than any other people that the LORD set his love on you and chose you, for you were the fewest of all peoples, but it is because the LORD loves you and is keeping the oath that he swore to your fathers. (Deut. 7:6–8)

Whenever the Bible addresses God's election, it always gives attention to God and underscores the unworthiness of those who have received his mercy.

In the New Testament, it is hard to ignore the emphasis on election, especially whenever salvation is mentioned. Believers are called God's "elect" or "chosen" ones (see Eph. 1:4; Col. 3:12; 1 Peter 1:1; 5:13). When evangelistic preaching led to conversions, Luke says, "As many as were appointed to eternal life believed" (Acts 13:48). Election took place "before the foundation of the world" (Eph. 1:4). In the case of Jacob and Esau, the Bible is very specific: "They were not yet born and had done nothing either good or bad—in order that God's purpose of election might continue, not because of works but because of him who calls" (Rom. 9:11). This verse is especially relevant, because, in addition to reinforcing the truth that election has nothing to do with human merit, it underscores the purpose of election: emphasizing the glory of the God who elects and calls sinners to saving faith.

The fact that election plays a central part in the Bible's account of salvation means it must also play a part in our own theology. George Whitefield, one of the great evangelists of the seventeenth century and a forerunner of the modern missionary movement, wrote, "I am persuaded, till a man comes to believe and feel these important truths [of election and the perseverance of the saints], he cannot come out of himself; but when convinced of these, and assured of the application of them to his own heart, he then walks by faith indeed, not in himself but in the Son of God, who died and gave himself for him. Love, not fear, constrains him to obedience."[1]

In this vein, Acts 18 draws a connection between knowledge of election and increased evangelistic fervor. The apostle Paul has been proclaiming Christ in Corinth and has already faced opposition and reviling. He has good reason to shy away from further gospel preaching, and his situation is about to get worse. In order to strengthen and embolden him, the Lord appears in a vision to remind him of the truths of election: "Do not be afraid, but go on speaking and do not be silent, for I am with you, and no one will attack you to harm you, for I have many in this city who are my people" (vv. 9–10). Paul's response is the same as that of so many faithful evangelists who understand God's sovereign work in salvation: he continues to preach the Word of God for another eighteen months, knowing his labor is not in vain.

Paul labored and suffered because of the truth of God's election. His words to his protégé Timothy in his last letter are especially striking in this regard:

> Remember Jesus Christ, risen from the dead, the offspring of David, as preached in my gospel, for which I am suffering, bound with chains as a criminal. But the word of God is not bound! Therefore I endure everything for the sake of the elect, that they also may obtain the salvation that is in Christ Jesus with eternal glory. (2 Tim. 2:8–10)

The connection that Paul makes between his endurance in proclaiming Christ and his knowledge of God's work in salvation, including election, is impossible to miss.

This connection did not originate in Paul's mind— Jesus taught the same thing. In John 6, Jesus offers himself to the crowds for their salvation. The context is significant. He uses an extended metaphor about himself, drawing on the Old Testament example of Moses: "I am the bread of life; whoever comes to me shall not hunger, and whoever believes in me shall never thirst" (v. 35). In saying this, Jesus expands on what he said earlier in the chapter about the work of God in their lives: "This is the work of God, that you believe in him whom he has sent" (v. 29).

As he offers himself to the people and urges them to trust in him, Jesus explains the spiritual dynamic at work. Here we must pay close attention to his words and follow their logic:

> But I said to you that you have seen me and yet do not believe. All that the Father gives me will come to me, and whoever comes to me I will never cast out. For I have come down from heaven, not to do my own will but the will of him who sent me. And this is the will of him who sent me, that I should lose nothing of all that he has given me, but raise it up on the last day. For this is the will of my Father, that everyone who looks on the Son and believes in him should have eternal life, and I will raise him up on the last day. (John 6:36–40)

Jesus declares here that his work of offering himself to the people, receiving those who come to him in faith, keeping them secure, and raising them up on the last day is linked with the Father's work in giving individuals to him. All who are given to Christ will come to him and believe.

This leads Jesus to make two further statements. First,

Jesus says, "No one can come to me unless the Father who sent me draws him. And I will raise him up on the last day" (John 6:44). Then he adds, "Truly, truly, I say to you, whoever believes has eternal life" (v. 47). The offer is free and made to all. Those who believe are received by Christ and kept to the end. But behind their salvation is the Father's eternal choice.

These are difficult concepts for us to understand now, just as they were difficult then. Perhaps it should comfort us to know that the first disciples wrestled with Jesus's teachings about salvation as well.

> When many of his disciples heard it, they said, "This is a hard saying; who can listen to it?" But Jesus, knowing in himself that his disciples were grumbling about this, said to them, "Do you take offense at this? Then what if you were to see the Son of Man ascending to where he was before? It is the Spirit who gives life; the flesh is no help at all. The words that I have spoken to you are spirit and life. But there are some of you who do not believe." (For Jesus knew from the beginning who those were who did not believe, and who it was who would betray him.) And he said, "This is why I told you that no one can come to me unless it is granted him by the Father." (John 6:60–65)

Is election a biblical doctrine? Our answer must be an emphatic yes! The Bible teaches that God's saving work is entrenched in his work of election. As we understand who God is and who we are as sinners, we realize that God must be the one who chooses and saves. If it were not so, we could not be saved. Because God has chosen who will be saved, we can and must proclaim the free offer of the gospel, knowing that God is at work in the world and bringing sinners to himself.

Questions for Further Reflection

1. Why is it so important for us to establish the authority of God's Word at the outset of our study of theology?

2. What objections are often raised to the doctrine of God's sovereignty? How does the Bible address these objections?

3. How does the doctrine of election magnify the grace of God in salvation? How does it spotlight human depravity?

4. How would you address the assertion that election is simply a doctrine taught by the Reformers and not by the Scriptures?

5. Why are those who believe in election often guilty of a failure to earnestly engage in personal evangelism? How does an understanding of election and God's sovereignty fuel the evangelistic enterprise?

3

THE COVENANTS

As we saw in the opening chapter, the reality of the covenant is deeply embedded in Scripture and vitally important to Reformed theology. In fact, throughout church history and even today, many use the terms *Reformed theology* and *covenant theology* interchangeably.

But what is a covenant? One helpful definition is "an agreement enacted between two parties in which one or both make promises under oath to perform or refrain from certain actions stipulated in advance."[1] Promises are made ahead of time in order to define the nature of the relationship.

The covenants provide the skeleton or structure for what God reveals about himself and for how he redeems his people. Robert Rollock, one of the great Scottish theologians of the 1500s, said that "God speaks nothing to man without the covenant."[2] Contemporary theologian J. I. Packer is no less bold: "First, the gospel of God is not properly understood till it is viewed in a covenantal frame. . . . Second, the word of God is not properly understood until it is viewed in a covenantal frame.... Third, the reality of God is not properly understood until it is viewed in a covenantal frame."[3] According to Rollock and Packer, all God's work in redemption is covenantal.

As we look at the Bible carefully, we can see that to be the case. The outworking of God's redemption is explained in terms of a covenant. In Reformed theology, the covenant of redemption is referred to as the *covenant of grace*. This overarching covenant is revealed in successive covenants in the Bible. Each of these needs to be explored in detail, but their unity under the covenant of grace should always be kept in view.

A Covenant of Works

We will begin again with Genesis. In Genesis 2:16–17, God gives his Word to Adam to govern and guide him. This revelation from God comes in the form of a covenant. As we have seen, it contains clear stipulations for Adam with warnings and blessings. In case we missed its covenantal structure, later in the Old Testament, when God rebukes Israel for unrepentant sin, he compares the nation to Adam in the garden of Eden: "Like Adam they transgressed the covenant; there they dealt faithlessly with me" (Hos. 6:7). What Hosea confirms is something that we can see for ourselves if we compare Genesis 2:16–17 with our definition of a covenant. The Lord gives his blessing, command, and promise to Adam in the form of a covenant. The relationship between the parties is defined, the obligations are clarified ahead of time, and the consequences are outlined.

The problem, of course, is that Adam does not keep the obligations of the covenant. Instead of obeying God's word and refraining from eating from the Tree of Knowledge of Good and Evil, Adam instead ignores God's word, follows his wife and the word of the serpent, and plunges mankind into ruin. This would only be undone in the glorious work of Christ, the last Adam. Paul puts it this way:

> For as by a man came death, by a man has come also the resurrection of the dead. For as in Adam all die, so also in Christ shall all be made alive. (1 Cor. 15:21–22)

God's revelation through a covenant does not begin and end with Adam's breaking of the covenant made in the garden. What we see after the fall of Adam is that God reveals his gracious plan of salvation in the form of successive covenants, all of which find their fulfillment in the work of the Lord Jesus Christ.

The Covenant with Noah

After the fall, the next covenant that is clearly identified as such is the covenant God makes with Noah and with every creature and human being to follow him (see Gen. 9:8–17). God has just destroyed the earth with a flood because of the wickedness of man, but he has rescued Noah and his family. In his covenant after this flood, God declares that, although human beings will continue in sin and rebellion against him, he will not destroy the earth with water again. He accompanies the covenant promise with a sign: a rainbow.

In a very real sense, the fact that God promises to withhold the judgment of a flood establishes the backdrop against which all the other covenant promises are fulfilled. God withholds this judgment because he plans to send his promised Son the Messiah to provide redemption for his people. To accomplish this salvation in Jesus Christ, God patiently and mercifully withholds judgment against sinners.

Everything else in the history of God's salvation has this kind covenant promise lying behind it; God will withhold universal judgment until the appointed day. It is the same logic we see when Peter writes about the ultimate salvation that will accompany Jesus's return. As Peter writes,

> The Lord is not slow to fulfill his promise as some count slowness, but is patient toward you, not wishing that any should perish, but that all should reach repentance. But the day of the Lord will come like a thief, and then the heavens will pass away with a roar, and the heavenly bodies will be burned up and dissolved, and the earth and the works that are done on it will be exposed. (2 Peter 3:9–10)

The Abrahamic Covenant

Having covenanted with humanity to withhold judgment for a time, God next reveals his salvation in a succession of major covenant promises. The first that we encounter is his promise to Abraham. As with the covenant with Noah, the parties are clearly identified; God gives a sign; and the covenant agreement applies to both a human representative and his descendants. The promise to Abraham is a promise of blessing. God promises to make his name great and, through Abraham, to bless all the families of the earth (see Gen. 12:2–3). As the covenant promise unfolds, we see that this blessing is realized in Abraham's offspring (see Gen. 15:3–5), reminding us of the promise made to Adam and Eve in Genesis 3:15. Later, God promises Abraham and his offspring a land (see Gen. 15; 17:8).

This covenant is embraced by Abraham through his faith. Genesis 15:6 records that Abraham "believed the LORD, and he counted it to him as righteousness" (v. 6). This covenant promise to Abraham also has a sign associated with it. In this case, the sign is male circumcision (see Gen. 17:10). The sign is to be applied to Abraham himself, since he has been brought into the covenant by God as an adult, but it is also for the males under his care, whether children or those brought into Abraham's house (see Gen. 17:13). This sign ultimately points to a greater reality and serves as a seal of the promise. Romans 4:11 says, "He received the sign of circumcision as a seal of the righteousness that he had by faith while he was still uncircumcised. The purpose was to make him the father of all who believe without being circumcised, so that righteousness would be counted to them as well."

This promise to Abraham is ultimately fulfilled in Christ (see Gal. 3:14) and is given to those in Christ: "If you are Christ's, then you are Abraham's offspring, heirs according to the promise" (Gal. 3:29). The covenant sign of circumcision also served its purpose, pointing to the need for a circumcision of the heart (see Deut. 10:16; 30:6; Jer. 4:4; 9:25). The New Testament puts it this way: "We are the circumcision, who worship by the Spirit of God and glory in Christ Jesus and put no confidence in the flesh" (Phil. 3:3).

The Sinai Covenant

The unfolding of God's salvation through the framework of the covenant is seen again in Exodus in the covenant God makes with the people through Moses. The specific time-bound obligations of this covenant are complex, and many relate specifically to the theocracy under which God's people lived. But the essence of the covenant is still gracious. Its background is God's work to redeem his people (see Ex. 19:4; Deut. 4:37; 7:7–9; 10:15).

The laws themselves have never been the means of salvation. The Bible considers this obvious: "Now it is evident that no one is justified before God by the law, for

'The righteous shall live by faith'" (Gal. 3:11). At the same time, the laws show what it means to live a holy life and also point forward to the ultimate redeeming work God will do through Christ. In this way, the covenant with Moses gives instruction about the nature and character of God, shows the holiness that God's people must exemplify when changed and empowered by his Spirit, and points to the work of God in the death of his Son as the perfect spotless sacrifice.

The Davidic Covenant

The next of our covenants comes in the account of David. In 2 Samuel 7, the Lord gives David rest from his enemies. Because of this, David desires to build a temple for him. Once again, God makes a covenant promise. Like the covenant with Abraham and the promises to Adam and Eve, this one centers on an offspring or seed of David.

When your days are fulfilled and you lie down with your fathers, I will raise up your offspring after you, who shall come from your body, and I will establish his kingdom. He shall build a house for my name, and I will establish the throne of his kingdom forever. I will be to him a father, and he shall be to me a son. When he commits iniquity, I will discipline him with the rod of men, with the stripes of the sons of men, but my steadfast love will not depart from him, as I took it from Saul, whom I put away from before you. And your house and your kingdom shall be made sure forever before me. Your throne shall be established forever. (2 Sam. 7:12–16)

This covenant promise to David has a near-term fulfillment in the life of Solomon, who builds the temple and with whom the Lord shows great patience. But the real promise goes far beyond Solomon. In Psalm 89, the psalmist says,

> You have said, "I have made a covenant with my
> chosen one;
>   I have sworn to David my servant:
> 'I will establish your offspring forever,
>   and build your throne for all generations.'"
>   (vv. 3–4)

This covenant promise of a king is central to God's plan of salvation, and it is the highlight of Gabriel's promise to Mary about her son:

> He will be great and will be called the Son of the Most High. And the Lord God will give to him the throne of his father David, and he will reign over the house of Jacob forever, and of his kingdom there will be no end. (Luke 1:32–33)

Each of the major turning points in God's revelation of salvation comes in the form of covenant promises. The words of J. I. Packer hold true: the gospel must be understood in a covenantal framework.

The New Covenant

The last major covenant revealed in the Bible is God's promise to give new spiritual life to his people so that they obey his commands. Jeremiah the prophet calls this promise a new covenant, Jesus refers to it as the new covenant, and the book of Hebrews, quoting from Jeremiah, does the same (see Jer. 31:31; Luke 22:20; Heb. 8:8–12).

Here is how Jeremiah explains this new covenant:

> Behold, the days are coming, declares the LORD, when I will make a new covenant with the house of Israel and the house of Judah, not like the covenant that I made with their fathers on the day when I took them by the hand to bring them out of the land of Egypt, my covenant that they broke, though I was their husband, declares the LORD. For this is the covenant that I will make with the house of Israel after those days, declares the LORD: I will put my law within them, and I will write it on their hearts. And I will be their God, and they shall be my people. And no longer shall each one teach his neighbor and each his brother, saying, "Know the LORD," for they shall all know me, from the least of them to the greatest, declares the LORD. For I will forgive their iniquity, and I will remember their sin no more. (Jer. 31:31–34)

While framing this as a covenant, Jeremiah echoes promises made by Moses in Deuteronomy 30. What God's people need is for him to transform them, to circumcise their hearts, to forgive their sins, and to change their hearts. This is part of God's revelation of his saving work. In Christ, he not only provides the promised blessing, the perfect sacrifice, and the eternal King but also transforms the hearts of his people and provides perfect forgiveness for sin.

Here is how the writer to Hebrews explains this:

> By a single offering he has perfected for all time those who are being sanctified.
>
> And the Holy Spirit also bears witness to us; for after saying,
>
>> "This is the covenant that I will make with them
>>   after those days, declares the Lord:
>> I will put my laws on their hearts,
>>   and write them on their minds,"
>
> then he adds,
>
>> "I will remember their sins and their lawless deeds
>> no more."
>
> Where there is forgiveness of these, there is no longer any offering for sin. (Heb. 10:14–18)

Later the author of Hebrews calls the atoning blood of Christ "the blood of the eternal covenant" (Heb. 13:20).

It is no surprise, given the significance of this covenant promise, that Jesus, on the night he was betrayed, spoke in similar terms: "This cup that is poured out for you is the new covenant in my blood" (Luke 22:20; see also 1 Cor. 11:25).

Understanding the covenantal structure of the Bible is vital to understanding the nature of Reformed theology. Because Reformed theology is centered on the Scriptures, the way in which the Bible reveals God's salvation must inform how we understand and proclaim it today. When we look carefully at the covenants as they unfold in Scripture, we not only see Jesus Christ more clearly but also see the breadth of God's salvation to all nations and the glories of a salvation that is by grace alone through faith alone in Christ alone—all to the glory of the triune God.

Questions for Further Reflection

1. What do we begin to see when we identify the covenantal structure of the Bible? What does the covenantal structure teach us about God?
2. What aspects of the redemptive work of Christ are highlighted by the Abrahamic, Mosaic, Davidic, and new covenants respectively?
3. What do God's covenants mean for you today?

4

THE BLESSINGS OF REFORMED THEOLOGY

The great truths of Reformed theology are a blessing to God's people. But why?

The Security of Scripture

First and most important, Reformed theology accurately represents what God has revealed about himself. The single most consequential question anyone can answer in life is "Who is God?" Reformed theology gives a clear and biblical answer.

Clarity about who God is and what he requires of his people is bound up in the notion of *sola Scriptura*, one of the key tenets of Reformed theology. Many today are convinced that they need to discern the will of God through a secret or subjective process. They work to generate inward emotional impressions, or they try to seek out an expert for advice. But Reformed theology points us back to the Bible. The Bible is where God clearly reveals himself and his will to us, and he does so in an intelligible way.

It is not just that what is revealed is clear; what is revealed is also authoritative. We can test other teachings against the teaching of the Bible. This too is a great blessing for us. Whenever we hear something taught about God or man, about the circumstances of life or the state of the world, we can test it against the authoritative standard of the Bible.

In emphasizing the Bible's role as the only authoritative source for our understanding of God and his will, Reformed theology also emphasizes the truths about God and salvation found most prominently in the Bible. These truths, and their emphasis in Reformed churches, have sometimes been disparaged. Sometimes even churches and theologians who come from a Reformed tradition downplay them. But as we will see, like the notion of the Bible's authority and clarity, each of these truths is a blessing.

The Comfort of God's Sovereignty

As we have seen already, God is sovereign over all aspects of our salvation. This is good news because the Bible teaches that, left to our own devices, we would have no hope of salvation. God is the one who elects in love and mercy; he is the one who draws sinners to himself; and he has committed himself to preserving those whom he has saved until the end. This is the thrust of the acronym TULIP, and it is the implication behind the five *solas*. Every facet of our salvation in Jesus Christ is a witness to the sinfulness of man, the sovereignty of God, the full provision of Christ, and the necessity of the work of the Holy Spirit. This is good news.

But one of the blessings of Reformed teaching is that it emphasizes not just the sovereignty of God in our salvation, but the sovereignty of God in all of life. This is good news, and it is a special comfort to us when times are difficult.

Any thinking person realizes that much of life is outside our control. Many of the most consequential events in our lives fall into this category. We do not decide when to be born. We cannot choose our parents. Although God often gives opportunities for learning and growth, some aspects of our physical and mental makeup will not change. Even the most health-conscious individual can face a shattering diagnosis or a crippling disease. Even where we seem to have the greatest influence, we encounter unintended consequences of our decisions and limitations to what we can accomplish. Although many value the illusion of control, an honest appraisal of our lives shows just how little power we have over them.

When things are going well, we can delude ourselves into believing that we are sovereign. Consider Nebuchadnezzar, who was walking along the rooftop of Babylon when he said, "Is not this great Babylon, which I have built by my mighty power as a royal residence and for the glory of my majesty?" (Dan. 4:30). This is the kind of madness to which we are susceptible in good times. We can convince ourselves that we are sovereign over all things and that our success, happiness, health, and friendships are evidence of our ability and control.

Suffering reveals the hollowness of these presumptions. It is through suffering that we become more aware of our weaknesses, our inability—in short, our lack of sovereignty. We realize that we are not in control.

This is a good place to start, and it is no coincidence that this is where Reformed theology teaches us to begin when it comes to salvation. The T in the famous TULIP acronym that some use to define a Reformed doctrine of salvation stands for *total depravity*. Understanding our salvation in Christ involves realizing the corruption of our nature. We must know our sinfulness and utter inability to save ourselves to fully appreciate the way God saves us.

This truth about salvation, which plays such a distinctive role in Reformed theology, points to a fact that applies to all of life: God is sovereign over all things. What a blessing to know this, especially as we suffer. Confronted with our weakness, we can turn to and trust in our loving Father. He is a God of mercy and compassion, and he is in control. Some believe that the world is ruled by competing forces or that our suffering means that God has lost his grip on the world or turned his back on his promises. Nothing could be further from the truth. In fact, when we surveyed the Bible's teaching on the crucifixion of Jesus Christ, we noted that the greatest undeserved suffering in human history was explicitly said to be according to God's pre-determined plan. God is sovereign even over the darkest moments, in control when we cannot help but realize we have no control at all.

God's sovereignty over all things extends from the small to the great. Nothing is beyond his care. Jesus reminds his followers of this.

> Are not two sparrows sold for a penny? And not one of them will fall to the ground apart from your Father. But even the hairs of your head are all numbered. Fear not, therefore; you are of more value than many sparrows. (Matt. 10:29–31)

What a blessing to have a theology that unapologetically emphasizes the absolute sovereignty of God! Jesus knew that nothing could be more comforting than this truth about God.

All of us, at one time or another, have looked at the state of the world and wondered—perhaps aloud, perhaps only to ourselves—why events were transpiring as they were. Maybe we have even approached the question from a personal perspective. Rather than asking why current events are unfolding as they are, we have wondered why our specific personal circumstances have happened as they have. These are difficult questions, and the Bible, let alone

Reformed theology, does not answer all of them. But the framework it provides nonetheless offers us great clarity.

The framework of Reformed theology reminds us that God is sovereign over everything that happens. The Westminster Confession of Faith, one of the great historical summaries of Reformed theology, puts it this way: "God from all eternity, did, by the most wise and holy counsel of his own will, freely, and unchangeably ordain whatsoever comes to pass."[1] Knowing this is a great comfort. Although it does not answer the particular questions we may have about one circumstance or another, it does remind us that every event and circumstance happens according to God's plan—even if they don't fit our own. Knowing this should eliminate many of the worries that consume our lives.

This encouragement from the sovereignty of God is compounded when we begin to appreciate the Bible's teaching on the goodness of God as a loving heavenly Father. It is possible to imagine a God who is entirely sovereign but who is not also good and wise and merciful. It is possible also to imagine God as loving and benevolent but fundamentally limited—or perhaps as thwarted by the designs of Satan or the decisions of man. But, as we have seen, the God of the Bible is shown to be both sovereign and good.

Look again at the statement from the Westminster Confession quoted above. The counsel of God's will is called "wise" and "holy," and so it is. This is exactly in keeping with what the whole of the Bible teaches.

Jesus, for example, teaches his disciples that knowing God as a good heavenly Father will keep them from undue anxiety. He links the sovereignty of God above all things with God's command for us to avoid anxiety (see Matt. 6:25–33). God's sovereignty and knowledge extends to birds and flowers and to what we need to eat and drink and wear. This does not inhibit our freedom, unless we define freedom as radical autonomy from God; rather, it enhances our freedom as creatures. We live with confidence knowing that he is both sovereign and good. Those who know God as Father know that his sovereignty coupled with his goodness is a blessing. It is our chief comfort.

This is the note struck by the first question of one of the great confessional documents of Reformed theology, the Heidelberg Catechism. The question is phrased this way: "What is your only comfort in life and death?" The answer is worth quoting in full:

> That I, with body and soul, both in life and death, am not my own but belong to my faithful Savior Jesus Christ, who with his precious blood has fully satisfied for all my sins and delivered me from all the power of the devil, and so preserves me that without the will of my heavenly Father not a hair can fall from my head; yea, that all things must be subservient to my salvation, wherefore by his Holy Spirit he also assures me of eternal life and makes me heartily willing and ready henceforth to live unto him.

This connection between the sovereignty of God and comfort extends beyond our personal lives. It provides a framework for making sense of God's purposes and work in the world. His purpose is to glorify himself, and in so doing he saves and works for the good of those whom he has called to himself.

In his Great Commission to his disciples, Jesus explicitly links his authority with the unstoppable work that he is doing through his people:

> All authority in heaven and on earth has been given to me. Go therefore and make disciples of all nations, baptizing them in the name of the Father and of the Son and of the Holy Spirit, teaching them to observe all that I have commanded you. And behold, I am with you always, to the end of the age. (Matt. 28:18–20)

This in no small measure shows what God is doing in the world. He is glorifying himself, bringing his children to conformity with Christ, and building Christ's church.

This understanding of God's work in the world puts everything in perspective. Whatever national or global events are transpiring, whatever challenges or dangers the church may face, Christians—especially those who preach and prize the sovereignty of God—know in an ultimate sense what God is doing. We can make sense of the world because we know that God is sovereign, that everything is according to his good plan and will.

The Wonder of God's Election

Closely tied to its emphasis on God's sovereignty is Reformed theology's undeniable emphasis on God's work in election. It may seem strange at first to call the doctrine of election a blessing. For many people, it is the first stumbling block they encounter in theology. Some look at the doctrine of election and believe that it is a gross violation of human freedom or that it is unfair and capricious or that it makes any human action irrelevant. But as we have seen, it is hard to argue with the biblical evidence. Although this can be hard teaching when we consider those close to us who do not believe, the doctrine of election is not merely something we should begrudgingly admit; rather, it is something we ought to embrace and celebrate. Although election is a mystery, it is ultimately a blessing for us to understand that God is the one who elects his people.

Why is that? There are several reasons. First, we must remember that we, by our nature, are sinners. We are bent away from God and are naturally at war with him. Because of our sin, we want our own way; we want to be in charge; we want to live according to our desires. This means that we would never choose God; we *could* never choose God. Submission to God and trust in his Son are fundamentally at odds with our nature as human beings. If God had not elected individuals out of his mercy and grace, then surely no one would be saved. We can rejoice in election because it points to the reality of God's great love for sinners.

Along with this, the doctrine of election is a blessing because it provides security for those who are saved. If we were left to ourselves, we would never choose God; and similarly, if it were up to us, our salvation would always be uncertain. What a blessing it is to read verses like Romans 8:30, in which Paul links predestination to glorification. Each is part of an unbreakable chain: "Those whom he predestined he also called, and those whom he called he also justified, and those whom he justified he also glorified." This unbreakable bond between predestination and glorification is a great comfort. God leaves no work unfinished or incomplete. His eternal act of predestination finally results in the glorification of those whom he has chosen. Real salvation always results in glorification. What a blessing this is! Salvation is not dependent on our changing moods but on God's unchanging plan, work, and choice.

And because of God's election, because he is the one who does the calling and it is his will that we are saved, we can also have security in our lives generally. What a blessing to have reminders of the relationship between God's work in salvation and his work in bringing all things for the good of his children and for their conformity to Christ:

> And we know that for those who love God all things work together for good, for those who are called according to his purpose. For those whom he foreknew he also predestined to be conformed to the image of his Son,

in order that he might be the firstborn among many brothers. (Rom. 8:28–29)

The Clarity of the Covenant

What are the blessings of understanding God as he is revealed through covenants? First, understanding the centrality of the covenant in the unfolding of God's purposes gives us a framework for understanding better the benefits of salvation. Imagine for a moment that you've just received a valuable gift as an inheritance. This life-changing gift offers tremendous benefits and privileges, and it would be natural for you to seek to understand it more fully. Or, to use another illustration, if you married into a new family or suddenly discovered a long-lost relative, you would likely want to learn how the story of your life fit in with the history and accomplishments of your extended relatives. Information about these relationships would surely be at a premium.

How much more should this be true of our salvation in Jesus Christ! The blessings that we receive in salvation are unfolded for us in the context of successive covenants. Only by studying and understanding those covenants can we truly begin to understand the blessings that come to us through Christ.

John Calvin reminds us that Jesus Christ comes "clothed with his gospel."[2] That gospel clothing is itself revealed to us in covenantal terms. Christ, as the summation and Mediator of these covenant blessings, is the one whom we should seek to know, understand, and worship more clearly. And God has revealed the person and benefits of Christ to us through his covenant promises. To understand what the covenants promise is to understand what Christ brings.

The covenants also remind us of the great continuity that exists among God's people from all generations. Believers in the time of the Old Testament were given a series of successive covenant promises, all of which displayed the unfolding drama of salvation that would be worked out in the life, death, resurrection, and ascension of Jesus Christ. In a very real sense, those who are in Christ today are spiritually connected to the covenant promises given in the past. This is why the apostle Paul can write, "And if you are Christ's, then you are Abraham's offspring, heirs according to promise" (Gal. 3:29). Reformed churches today often describe themselves as a "covenant community." This shows both our connection with one another and our connection with those members of God's covenant people from the past.

For this same reason, when the apostle Paul sought to remind Christians of the spiritual dangers they faced, he looked back to the nation of Israel at the time of the Exodus, writing, "For I do not want you to be unaware, brothers, that our fathers were all under the cloud, and all passed through the sea" (1 Cor. 10:1). Even though Paul is writing to gentile Christians, he refers to those who were rescued from Egyptian slavery as *our fathers*. These verses make it clear that the covenants bind our experience to those of the past.

The emphasis within Reformed theology on the covenants also reminds us of promises and warnings God has given to those who will come after us. It is no accident that historically Reformed churches emphasize the blessing of children and the responsibilities of children to parents and parents to children. This has to do with the solidarity of those who are part of God's visible covenant community. We can see this proclaimed on the day of Pentecost in Peter's great sermon. There, Peter declared that the promises of salvation along with the command of repentance are offered by God freely to all who heard. But Peter adds, "The promise is for you and for your children and for all who are far off, everyone whom the Lord our God calls to himself" (Acts 2:39).

When looking at the example of God's people in the Old Testament, we cannot help but notice that parents play a significant role in passing along to their children either a vibrant commitment to the Lord and his Word or a relative indifference and spirit of compromise. Reformed theology and its emphasis on the importance of God's operation by means of a covenant underscores this reality. Believers not only have personal spiritual obligations but are commanded to say along with Joshua, "As for me and my house, we will serve the LORD" (Josh. 24:15). This is an application of the commands given by God in

Deuteronomy 6:4–9 for parents to teach their children his commands "when you sit in your house, and when you walk by the way, and when you lie down and when you rise" (v. 7). Households have these responsibilities because of the nature of God's covenant promises, which were offered to God's people and their children, household by household. Although every individual is called to personal repentance and faith in Christ, our lives as believers are never simply a solo mission. We come out of families, many of us are called to lead as parents, and we walk in faith as part of a larger covenant community.

This larger covenant community is the church. It is a community grounded in a covenant. We can see this by looking at the two sacraments Jesus Christ gave to his church. Both of them—baptism and the Lord's Supper—are covenant signs and seals. Baptism is the covenant sign of new birth. Its symbolism points to the washing work of the Holy Spirit, and it welcomes all who receive it into God's visible family, challenging them with the obligation of repentance and belief in the Lord Jesus Christ for salvation from sin. The Lord's Supper is grounded in Christ's work on the cross. Symbolically, it points to the body and blood of Christ, and it is a seal of the promises established in that substitutionary death. This is why Jesus Christ, in establishing this supper, calls the cup "the new covenant in my blood" (Luke 22:20). We also see that Jesus Christ, by the Holy Spirit, has fellowship with his people as they partake of this covenant meal (see 1 Cor. 10).

The centrality of the covenant when it comes to our salvation has tremendous implications for us. It gives us clarity in our understanding of God's saving purposes; it binds us together with believers from past eras, even those who lived before the decisive revelation of Jesus Christ; it gives us a framework for understanding God's work in the family and our lives as Christians in the church. Although covenant theology may be downplayed or denied among some Christians, Reformed Christianity has always emphasized it. It is one of the identifying marks of Reformed theology, and the expression of it is a blessing to be both embraced and proclaimed.

Transparency in Our Confession

One of the features of Reformed theology that we introduced in the opening chapter is its commitment to robust and thorough public confessions of faith. It is appropriate for us to examine it after evaluating the great blessings of covenant theology, since the covenant community of the church is visibly defined by its commitment to a confession of faith.

Historically, even in times of great persecution, churches in the Reformed tradition invested significantly in formulating public confessions to declare what they believed. Most of the time, these confessions of faith were accompanied by catechisms for teaching children and those who were new to the faith. As we have noted, this impulse to teach or catechize the next generation also fits with Reformed theology's emphasis on the covenantal realities of our salvation in Jesus Christ.

As a practical matter, when confessions are abandoned or ignored, then the other distinguishing features of Reformed theology—including its emphasis on the central authority of Scripture—almost immediately decline as well. That is why confessions of faith, while never taking the place of Scripture in terms of authority, are taken so seriously.

Another benefit of confessions of faith is that they offer transparency to those within the church and to those outside it. By them we proclaim that we believe that the Bible declares certain things to be true about God, humanity, salvation, the church, and the world. This kind of clarity and integrity—what might in the business world be called "truth in advertising"—should be a priority for all Christians, and especially for Christian ministers. Proverbs teaches us that God "is a shield to those who walk in integrity" (Prov. 2:7). We know that God blesses those who openly state the truth: "The righteous who walks in his integrity—blessed are his children after him" (Prov. 20:7).

We see this exemplified in the ministry of the apostle Paul, who writes, "For our boast is this, the testimony of our conscience, that we behaved in the world with simplicity and godly sincerity, not by earthly wisdom but by the grace of God, and supremely so toward you" (2 Cor. 1:12). He contrasts his ministry with others along these same lines: "For we are not, like so many, peddlers of God's word, but as men of sincerity, as commissioned by God, in the sight of God we speak in Christ" (2 Cor. 2:17). Part of this kind of sincerity and integrity involves stating clearly what you believe and are committed to teaching—to *confessing* the faith that you hold. Then, after confessing it with clarity, holding on to it with integrity.

Clear confessions of this kind have always accompanied the healthiest and truest expressions of Reformed theology. They are a way of proclaiming to the world what the church believes; of training the next generation in the essential elements of the faith; and of guiding those in the church as they evaluate any teaching or practice that they might encounter. The history of the church shows us that no enduring expression of Reformed teaching is possible without creeds and confessions of faith. And given the benefits of such confessions, what reason could we possibly have for wanting to ignore them?

In all this, we must acknowledge that confessions of faith are, by their very nature, limiting. This may be the reason that many churches and individuals today reject the use of historical confessions. After all, if you are clear about the Bible's teaching on election, then you are saying that other views are incorrect. If you declare yourself on an issue such as baptism, then you are also declaring that the Bible speaks to these matters and does so in a binding way. To be presbyterian in your form of church government means that you will not be exclusively congregational nor will you be episcopal.

The fact that confessions bind in this way makes some people uneasy. Many wish to have churches free from these kinds of restrictions. Even within denominations committed nominally to a confession, many chafe under the perceived restrictiveness of clear doctrinal conclusions. Three brief points need to be made in answer to these objections.

First, the Bible itself assumes the need for doctrinal statements or public confessions of faith. This is what Paul describes when writing to Timothy. He wrote, "Follow the pattern of the sound words that you have heard from me, in the faith and love that are in Christ Jesus" (2 Tim. 1:13). It is elsewhere referred to as a "standard of teaching" (Rom. 6:17). In the Old Testament, we see clear creedal statements in such places as Deuteronomy 6:4: "Hear O Israel: the LORD our God, the LORD is one." If the Bible assumes that there are creedal commitments to which we must be committed, then surely we must take this seriously.

But second, historical confessions carry with them the benefits of age and seasoned reflection. We should not ever imagine that we, alone with our Bibles and our limited range of experiences, would not benefit from the counsel and teaching of others. There is wisdom in a multitude of counselors, and often (though not always!) teachings that stand the test of time and scrutiny should be given great weight in our consideration. We should be troubled and concerned by an attitude that suggests that everyone else has gotten it wrong and that our church is the first to read the Bible clearly. A Christian finds stability in committing to a confession. A confession must never take precedence over the Bible, of course, but it can act as a guardrail against the potential of abuse and manipulation by those who claim to have discovered the truth for the first time.

Finally, as we have seen, confessions have the benefit of declaring our beliefs in clear and balanced ways to those who are watching. Within the church, they bind us to a certain kind of teaching and prevent one person from assuming absolute and new authority. In the world, they let others know exactly what we teach and why, without any spin, guile, or obfuscation. As we have seen, these are not just virtues, they are requirements of a ministry patterned after the New Testament.

Is Reformed Theology a Blessing?

Our contention here is that we can not only define and defend Reformed theology but also embrace and celebrate it. Any areas that at first glance may appear to be liabilities are actually assets. The authority of the Bible, the sovereignty and election of God, the clarity of the covenants, and the transparency and accountability of public confessions are all good gifts. The Scriptures are clear about the central authority of God's Word and on the absolute sovereignty of God in all of life—especially in salvation. Covenants are vital to the work of God, and robust public confession, while antithetical to our modern notions of independence and autonomy, gives us the stable conditions we need for ministry and evangelism in our modern world.

These central distinctions between Reformed theology and other theological systems should not be blurred or ignored. Reformed theology, with its adherence to the grand truths of Scripture, is a ballast and blessing to Christians seeking a strong foundation and a coherent framework for their faith.

Questions for Further Reflection

1. In what ways is God's sovereignty a special comfort in the midst of suffering?
2. How does God's sovereignty in salvation give us confidence when we look to the future?
3. Why is it such a blessing that God has revealed his salvation in the covenants?
4. How do unbelievers benefit from the transparency provided by creeds and confessions? How do these same creeds benefit Christians within the church?

QUESTIONS AND ANSWERS
ON REFORMED THEOLOGY

In the following pages you will find questions with short answers—at least, answers as short as I could muster. Reformed theology raises a myriad of questions from various quarters. This chapter does not address every question that could be asked, and so there is a list of recommended resources for further reading at the end of this book.

Do I need to understand theology to know God more deeply?

Theology just means "words about God," "ideas about God," or "the study of God." In that sense, everyone is a theologian. A person might be a bad theologian or a careless theologian or a heretical theologian, but nearly everyone has some idea about God and the teachings connected to God. So in a basic sense, knowing God is irreducibly linked to understanding theology correctly.

But often when this question is asked, what the questioner really means is something like "Do I have to read books on theology or study theology in an academic set-ting in order to know God?" The answer to that question is no, but it is a qualified no. The reason we must qualify what we say is that when the Bible speaks about growing in the grace of God, it couples growing in the grace of God with growth in the knowledge of God.

Just like with any other relationship in our lives, it would be nonsensical for us to think we could grow in the knowledge of God without knowing more about him. We must listen to what he says in the Bible; we must study and ponder the works of the Lord; and we must not be merely hearers but also doers of his Word. It is worth noting that Peter, in his last words to the church, couples growth in grace with growth in *knowledge* (see 2 Peter 3:18).

However, although there is a significant temptation to separate study and meditation from a knowledge of God, there can be an equal or greater danger of thinking that because we say the right words about Christ, therefore we know him. We can also delude ourselves into thinking that because we do things in the name of Christ, therefore we know him. Jesus warns against this when he says,

> On that day many will say to me, "Lord, Lord, did we not prophesy in your name, and cast out demons in your name, and do many mighty works in your name?" And then will I declare to them, "I never knew you; depart from me, you workers of lawlessness." (Matt. 7:22–23)

The warning Jesus gives here is to those who knew what to call him, and who knew the kind of works he desired, but who did not know him.

We can approach Jesus Christ only on his terms, acknowledging our sin and repenting of it, trusting in him alone for our salvation—not in something we call him or in something we have done. That is the beginning of true knowledge of Christ.

How does Reformed theology affect my reading of the New Testament?

Reformed theology, rightly understood, emerges from the study of the whole Bible, both Old and New Testaments. But the system that emerges from our study of the Bible also helps us to see New Testament truths that we otherwise might have missed. For instance, once we see that the whole Bible both displays and declares the absolute sovereignty of God in salvation, we begin to understand why Christians are referred to repeatedly in the New Testament as "chosen ones" or "the elect of God." This same understanding of God's sovereignty can help us to read New Testament books like Acts more sensitively. When reading, we know that all that is being carried out is according to God's predetermination. Nothing is outside his control. He is in charge at all times, and his plan is being carried out for his glory.

On a slightly more nuanced level, understanding the continuity between God's covenant promises in the Old Testament and the New Testament provides a helpful perspective on what it means to live as a Christian and to be part of a church. As we have seen, the New Testament shows the great continuity between the people of God in the Old and New Testaments.

How does infant baptism fit with Reformed theology? Do I have to believe in infant baptism to be Reformed?

Infant baptism is related to the emphasis in Reformed theology on the covenants. In the Old Testament, one of the signs and seals of the covenant was circumcision. Circumcision was part of the covenant with Abraham. It was performed on every male convert (to show their trust in God) and on their male children (to show the ongoing offer and work of God in the next generation).

In most expressions of Reformed theology, this sign and seal is believed to have carried over into baptism, which is administered to all new converts and the children, both male and female, of Christians. Like circumcision, which identifies recipients with God and signifies the work of God on the heart and calls people to repentance and faith, baptism identifies recipients with God, signifies the cleansing and renewing ministry of God in the hearts of his people, and calls both recipients of baptism and those observing this visible sign to repentance and faith.

Because of the continuity of the covenants and the logic of the sign and seal, most within the Reformed tradition see the baptism of believers and their children as the most biblical expression of baptism. However, the specific nature of how God's covenant is administered is debated within Reformed theology. Although there has historically been wide consensus that both believers and their children are members of God's covenant people, since the 1600s, some have embraced some of the distinctives indicated by the label *Reformed* but simultaneously questioned how the children of believers relate to God's covenant promises and warnings. These Christians refer to themselves today as Reformed Baptists.

Some argue that Reformed Baptists should not be classified as Reformed since the idea of the covenant plays such a significant role in our definition of Reformed theology, especially when it comes to our understanding of the sacraments and ecclesiology. We cannot carelessly ignore the implications of these debates, but at the same time there is wide common ground shared by those who emphasize the reality of God's work in and through the covenants and in salvation.

Is Reformed theology just something for those who are intellectual?

Not at all. Historically, Reformed churches have emerged among what we would think of as regular people. Although there are exceptions, most of the historic Reformed churches have not received immediate support from nobles or intellectuals.

This makes sense because Reformed theology is simply a restatement of the Bible's teaching on authority, the nature of man and salvation, and the purpose of God's work in the world. It has always emphasized teaching these truths to the next generation and involving children in the life of the local church. At its best, Reformed theology is designed for discipleship: theologically robust and arising clearly from the text of Scripture.

However, it must be said that many today who use the label Reformed or who discover Reformed theology find it intellectually stimulating and satisfying. For some, Reformed teaching answers basic questions and opens vistas for further intellectual exploration. This is a wonderful thing. Reformed churches have always insisted that pastors be educated and skilled in sound doctrine, and the best theologians in the Reformed tradition have tried to engage with the leading intellectual movements of their day. They do so drawing on a clear and realistic understanding of the nature of man and the sovereignty of our Creator God.

This means that Reformed theology can offer someone who is intellectually inclined much to study and talk about. At its core, though, Reformed theology is a balanced and thoughtful declaration of the teaching of Scripture. It is meant to shape lives and cultivate churches that are centered on the glorious gospel of the Lord Jesus Christ. It is a theology for life—not just the life of the mind, but the life of the whole person dedicated to God completely.

What does Reformed theology teach about the Holy Spirit?

One of the most surprising criticisms of Reformed theology is that it has an underdeveloped doctrine of the Holy Spirit. Some even suggest that to be Reformed is to deny the ministry of the Holy Spirit altogether. Nothing is further from the truth! John Calvin has been called the theologian of the Holy Spirit, and most Reformed theologians who have followed him have learned from his priorities. An emphasis on the Holy Spirit, far from being foreign to Reformed theology, is near to its vital center. A brief survey of the Puritan theologians in England and in North America reveals a clear emphasis on the need for the Holy Spirit and a study of the doctrine of the Holy Spirit.

Part of the reason for this is Reformed theology's teaching on the depravity of man. Because man is sinful by nature and totally unable to save himself, new birth by the Holy Spirit is an essential component of salvation. The Holy Spirit must give new life to someone who is spiritually dead. This same emphasis is found in the Reformed doctrine of sanctification, which stresses the work of the Holy Spirit in transforming sinful believers more and more into the image of Jesus Christ.

One of the reasons that Reformed theology is not as closely associated with the doctrine of the Holy Spirit today is because of the rise of the modern charismatic and Pentecostal movements. These movements emphasize the so-called miraculous gifts of the Spirit, especially speaking in tongues and prophecy. Mainstream Reformed theology has always understood these phenomena to be associated with the unique apostolic ministry in the earliest years of the church. We would note, for instance, that nowhere are either of these gifts mentioned in the pastoral epistles, which give normative instruction for the church and pastoral ministry. Even in the book of Acts, their practice wanes as the book progresses.

By the recent standard of Pentecostalism, it might appear that Reformed theology has less to say about the Holy Spirit, but when viewed from the standpoint of history, and when evaluated in light of the balanced biblical teaching on the subject, Reformed theology not only joyfully embraces the ministry of the Holy Spirit but positively emphasizes it.

Many people who claim to be Reformed are prickly or obnoxious. Why is this?

As with any theological system, those who embrace Reformed theology are not always known for their humility or winsomeness. The popular term *cage-stage Calvinist* describes many who embrace the doctrines of grace for the first time.

Some of this can be chalked up to the pitfalls of youth. It is worth remembering that the apostle Paul warned against youthful passions. Immediately following this he wrote, "Have nothing to do with foolish, ignorant controversies; you know that they breed quarrels. And the Lord's servant must not be quarrelsome" (2 Tim. 2:23–24). Sadly, it has always been the case that those who are new to the faith, or who are new in their embrace of a biblical truth, are prone to become quarrelsome because of it.

Those who understand some of the basic truths of Reformed theology should be most able to diagnose the problem with those who are prickly and obnoxious about their doctrinal commitments. We know that human beings are selfish and egotistical by nature, prone to take credit for things they did not earn and to boast in their own supposed superiority to others. All of this is especially egregious when understood in light of the doctrines of grace. If there is one thing that should make us all joyful and humble, it is meditating on the free and undeserved favor we have received in the Lord Jesus Christ, by grace alone through faith alone.

What the apostle Paul says should be repeated to all who use their newfound understanding of theology in a way that elevates themselves or smacks of pride: "What do you have that you did not receive? If then you received it, why do you boast as if you did not receive it?" (1 Cor. 4:7). This verse summarizes the big idea behind the five *solas* as well as the five points of Calvinism: What do you have that you did not receive? The depravity of man explains why those who claim to be Reformed are argumentative or arrogant, but the fact that they are so reveals that, despite labeling themselves Reformed, they know little of the truths to which they so confidently attest.

Doesn't Reformed theology deny free will? Does it make human beings into robots?

The sovereignty of God is prominent in Reformed theology. We emphasize, first, that God is sovereign in all salvation, but also that he is entirely sovereign over all things that come to pass. This raises the question of human free will. In Reformed theology, are human beings really free?

There are a few answers to this question. First, Reformed theology teaches that free will itself is downstream from the notion of the heart or the affections. In other words, we choose that which we love; we are driven by that which we desire. So in trying to understand human beings, the questions we should be asking are, How are our desires shaped and formed? On what do we set our affections and why? Desires drive choices.

Those questions have clear biblical answers that are highlighted by Reformed theology. Human beings, by nature, are bent away from God. We are led by selfish desires. This is why, in the introduction to his glorious words about salvation by grace through faith, Paul writes about our state apart from Christ: "We all once lived in the passions of our flesh, carrying out the desires of the body and the mind, and were by nature children of wrath, like the rest of mankind" (Eph. 2:3). When it comes to human choices, Reformed theology has a clear answer that addresses not just our capacity to choose (what most mean by free will) but the much more important question of why we choose as we do. This is why there is an emphasis not only on the depravity of man but also on the need for new birth by the Holy Spirit.

Reformed theology is also clear that human beings are accountable for their actions. A judgment day is coming, and God commands us all to repent and believe the gospel and to obey his commands (see Acts 17:30). But while all human beings are held accountable, God is in control. He is working all things according to the counsel of his will. Even the freely chosen sinful actions of those whose desires are in opposition to God are used by God for good. The words of Joseph in response to his brothers' sin against him will one day be said to all those who oppose God and reject his revelation: "You meant evil against me, but God meant it for good" (Gen. 50:20).

Doesn't Reformed theology de-emphasize missions and evangelism?

Sadly, many Christians give little thought to the reality of hell and to the mission Christ gave to his church to go and make disciples of all nations (see Matt. 28:19). This is not confined to Reformed churches, which, historically, have been among the most fervent in sending missionaries and evangelists.

Reformed theology should give great confidence to those who are obeying God's call to evangelize and who support the church's work of missions. We know that salvation is entirely a work of God and that the same God who ordains the end (salvation) also ordains the means (the proclamation of God's Word). This is the precise logic used in Romans 10. After one of the clearest descriptions of the nature and purpose of election in Romans 9, Paul writes,

> How then will they call on him in whom they have not believed? And how are they to believe in him of whom they have never heard? And how are they to hear without someone preaching? And how are they to preach unless they are sent? As it is written, "How beautiful are the feet of those who preach the good news!" (Rom. 10:14–15)

Paul's understanding of God's work in salvation did not detract from his missionary zeal. It fueled it.

We see this on display in the book of Acts. In Acts 13, Paul and Barnabas preach to both Jews and gentiles. When they preach to the gentiles, wonderful things happen: "When the Gentiles heard this, they began rejoicing and glorifying the word of the Lord, and as many as were appointed to eternal life believed" (Acts 13:48). God used the preaching of the Word to bring many to salvation.

This same dynamic is at work in individual evangelism. In Philippi, a wealthy woman named Lydia heard the message of the gospel, and "the Lord opened her heart to pay attention to what was said by Paul" (Acts 16:14).

The teaching of Reformed theology brings confidence to those who engage in the work of evangelism. It reminds us of the authority and power of the Bible alone (*sola Scriptura*); it emphasizes the gracious nature of salvation (*sola gratia, sola fide*) and of the focus of our proclamation (*solus Christus*). And because it is God who ultimately appoints people to eternal life and opens their hearts to respond, we know that all our efforts are to his glory alone (*soli Deo gloria*).

What if I like Reformed theology's tenets in some areas but not in others? Am I Reformed?

This takes us back to the question of definition. Reformed theology has been defined in different ways by different teachers. The definition provided in this book is a fairly mainstream, middle-of-the-road definition. If you have major objections to what is described here, then perhaps *Reformed* is not the best label for your theological system.

The far bigger question is whether or not your views fit with the Bible and whether they cohere together in a reasonable and logical way. Be certain that the standard of authority for your convictions is the Bible alone. Then look carefully at the Scriptures and compare your conclusions with the conclusions of God's Word. You may find biblical ideas that you do not like or that do not fit neatly with what you've been taught in the past. Submit to the authority of God's Word. This is what Reformed theology seeks to do.

It is also important to ask whether the views that you hold are contradictory not only to the direct teaching of Scripture but also to the logic of the Scriptures. One example of this relates to the sovereignty of God. Some freely confess that God is in control of all things, but they also maintain that God cannot choose anyone for salvation, because to do so would violate a sacred principle of human freedom. In this case, we would say that the denial not only contradicts clear biblical teaching on the nature of God's work in salvation but also does not fit in any reasonable way with the notion of God's total sovereignty. Examples like this could be multiplied, but one of the most compelling features of Reformed theology is that it not only represents the teaching of Scripture but also fits together coherently. This is exactly what we would expect because God is a God of order, and it is also one thing that we should look for in evaluating our theological conclusions.

What if I am convinced of Reformed theology but don't belong to a Reformed church? What is the importance of the local church to Reformed theology?

It is hard to overstate the importance of the church to Reformed theology. Reformed theology finds its expression not just in individual minds but also in covenantal congregations that worship God and sit under his Word, are strengthened by Christ's sacraments, and carry out his commission to his people. This is where all the truths associated with Reformed theology can be seen on display. In Reformed theology, Jesus Christ is proclaimed as the head of the church.

Therefore, a church that is truly Reformed will, first and foremost, submit to the leadership of Jesus Christ that is given in his Word. Biblical instruction ought to govern every aspect of church life. The regular preaching of God's Word, which is sadly absent from many churches today, must take its place at the center of public worship. The administration of the sacraments of baptism and communion are to be conducted by the Word of God.

Reformed churches will strive to conduct all public worship in accord with the Word of God as well. What happens in the worship of God must be regulated by what God himself has commanded. He has taught his people how he is to be approached, and the Bible is clear that all worship must be done with joyful and faithful reverence and awe (see Heb. 12:28).

Even the way the church is organized ought to be determined by biblical teaching and example. This is known as the *polity* of the church, and it addresses things such as the role of church officers (elders and deacons), the kinds of decisions made by congregations, and the nature of church membership.

All this underscores the fact that the church is the visible covenant community of God today. It is overseen by Christ, indwelt by God's Holy Spirit, and made up of a people dedicated to the Triune God of creation. Every feature that we have outlined related to Reformed theology—from the truths of God's sovereignty to the nature of the covenant to the adherence to public confessions of faith—all of it finds its expression in the church of Jesus Christ, guided and governed by the authority of the Word of God.

How do I find a Reformed church?

The answer to this question may depend on your context. In some situations, you may be able to look up a church by its association with a denomination that is confessionally Reformed and committed to the authority of the Bible. This is a good place to start. When looking at the information provided by a given church, you may be able to discern its view of the Bible and see if it adheres to a historic public confession of faith such as the Westminster Confession of Faith or the Three Forms of Unity. Several online databases compile information on churches that meet these criteria.

You may need to visit these churches, particularly if several publicly identify with these historic Reformed confessions. When visiting, think carefully about the approach to God's authority that the church takes. Is every aspect of church life—preaching, teaching, worship, sacraments, leadership—governed and guided by God's Word? This is the starting place of Reformed theology, and it is the mark of any church that fits with the definition of Reformed offered in this book.

How does Reformed theology affect my view of worship?

Reformed theology has a high view of God. He is the sovereign Creator of all things, and he rules over his creation. This should provoke us to praise him in a way that acknowledges his holiness. Because God is so majestic, so powerful, so great, our praise to him ought to reflect this. The Bible says, "Great is the LORD, and greatly to be praised" (Ps. 145:3).

Reformed worship of God should also be joyful because of our acknowledgment that salvation is a gift from God from beginning to end. When we approach God in worship, we do so because of what he has done for us in Jesus Christ. Our worship is acceptable only because of Christ's sacrifice and because of his ministry as our Great High Priest. We can sing and speak and hear from God because of the ministry of his Holy Spirit. Life itself, and spiritual life in particular, is all a gift from God.

Since it is God who takes the initiative, this principle is reflected in the worship of Reformed churches. Traditional Reformed worship is *dialogical*, meaning God and the worshippers are in a kind of conversation. But the agenda for the conversation is set by God's declarations. This is why, traditionally, Reformed worship begins with a call to worship and ends with a benediction. God gets the first word and the last word. Our singing, confession, and prayers are a response to God's Word.

God's Word also takes center stage in the high point of a Reformed service, which is the preaching of the Word of God. At this time, God's people, who have gathered to worship their great God, hear from him with clarity as an ordained minister of the gospel opens the Word of God and instructs and exhorts from it.

Some see this dialogical approach as repetitive. Indeed, many have observed that most Reformed worship services have a similar shape and feel to them. This is true, but it is worth remembering why it is true. It is not because Reformed churches are beholden to tradition. Rather, it is because they are bound by the Word of God. This commitment to allowing God's Word alone to govern how God is worshipped—not adding to it or subtracting from it—is vital, and is often called the regulative principle of worship. Reformed churches are governed by the one Jesus Christ. They are worshipping the same God who revealed his will in the Bible. They see the same elements of worship when they read the Bible, and they know that they dare not add to those with their invented ideas. To commune with God, we must come on his terms, responding to what he says and submitting our will to his. Novelty is not our goal; meeting with God is.

What a privilege it is to have God's Word! What a joy to be governed by Jesus Christ and guided by the Holy Spirit!

Isn't Reformed worship like Roman Catholic worship?

Although some may see the relative seriousness of traditional Reformed worship and associate it with Roman Catholicism, the principles of Reformed worship emerged in the 1600s in direct opposition to Roman Catholic worship. In Roman Catholic worship, the centerpiece is the bread and wine. These elements are presented as having changed into the actual body and blood of Jesus Christ through transubstantiation. These elements are said to confer grace to those who partake and are an essential part of an individual's salvation. In Roman Catholic teaching, assurance of salvation cannot be achieved in this life. Good works commingle and respond to God's grace in a meritorious way, and the undergirding authority structure of Roman worship is ultimately connected to the authority of the pope and those ordained officially by the church.

Reformed worship is entirely different. Its authority is found in Jesus Christ and is revealed in his Word. Because of this, the centerpiece of Reformed worship is the reading and preaching of the Word of God. Our worship is acceptable to God through Christ and we come to worship because he has promised forgiveness and acceptance to those who approach him through faith. Reformed worship celebrates the Lord's Supper, recognizing that Jesus Christ communes with his people and strengthens them in and through it by his Holy Spirit— not materially, but spiritually. This supper, as significant as it is, is conducted as a ministry of the Word of God. That is why Reformed pastors are ordained to the ministry of Word and sacrament.

The Word of God is what governs Reformed worship. It is from that Word that we derive our principles and our preaching. It is according to that Word that we conduct our praise and prayer. It is because of that Word that we proclaim the free offer of the gospel to all, by grace alone, through faith alone, in Christ alone.

How does Reformed theology affect my family?

We have already noted the emphasis in Reformed theology on the covenants of Scripture. These covenants show us the work of Christ and how God administers salvation by grace to those whom he has called to himself. These covenants not only tie us to the past and give obligations for the present; they also give an offer of grace to future generations. This is why Reformed churches include children as recipients of the covenant sign and instruct them in the promises of God for those who believe and the warnings of those who ignore God's call to repentance and faith.

Those who have understood this best have emphasized the need to train children in how to approach God in worship. This is why many Reformed churches encourage children to remain in the worship service. There is also great emphasis placed on catechesis—training in theology through simple questions and answers. All these training methods have been a part of the Reformed tradition since its earliest days.

Another feature of the Reformed tradition is that of family worship. Although this takes shape differently from family to family (and often depends on the age of the children involved), the idea is that parents (ideally fathers) will lead their children in daily Bible reading and instruction and prayer. Some parents also lead their children in singing. This family worship usually takes only a short time, but it comes from taking seriously the biblical commands to parents. The Bible teaches that Christian fathers and mothers should model submission to the Lord, should instruct their children in the things of God, and are to put before them their obligations and opportunities as members of his covenant community.

One of the wonderful privileges of living as a Christian is to see God change not just individual lives in saving them, but also to see the Lord work through entire families, transforming marriages, saving children, bringing a whole household under the authority of the Word and the protection of the Son.

RECOMMENDED RESOURCES

Boice, James M. *Whatever Happened to the Gospel of Grace? Rediscovering the Doctrines That Shook the World*. Wheaton: Crossway, 2009. First published in 2001. [This is a readable introduction to the five *solas* of the Reformation. It includes a diagnosis of the ways in which these truths are ignored or sidelined in many evangelical churches and is a stirring call to recover their centrality.]

Boice, James M. and Phillip G. Ryken. *The Doctrines of Grace: Rediscovering the Evangelical Gospel*. Wheaton: Crossway, 2009. First published in 2002. [Similar to the text above, this one is concerned with the five points of Calvinism. It provides a biblical argument for each of these truths of salvation and shows how they fit together to give a full-orbed portrait of the redemption accomplished by Jesus Christ.]

Fesko, J. V. *Word, Water, and Spirit: A Reformed Perspective on Baptism*. Grand Rapids: Reformation Heritage Books, 2021. [Fesko provides both a historical and a biblical argument for the Reformed doctrine of infant baptism. While it may require some careful reading, his book is nonetheless clear and comprehensive.]

Meyers, Stephen G. *God to Us: Covenant Theology in Scripture*. Grand Rapids: Reformation Heritage Books, 2021. [An in-depth study of each of the covenants of Scripture and how they fit together as a whole. It is best read with a Bible in hand but is thoroughly conversant with the best Reformed sources of the past.]

Murray, John. *Redemption Accomplished and Applied*. 1955. New edition with foreword by Carl R. Trueman. Grand Rapids: Eerdmans, 2015. [A classic introduction to the doctrine of salvation. Murray is clear and biblical, and he does an especially fine job of highlighting the central importance of union with Jesus Christ and of the applying work of the Holy Spirit.]

Rhodes, Jonty. *Covenants Made Simple: Understanding God's Unfolding Promises to His People*. Phillipsburg, NJ: P&R Publishing, 2014. [A simple and clear introduction to covenant theology. It is not intended to give detail or to interact with scholarly sources, but it does nicely summarize some of the key features of the biblical portrayal of the covenants.]

Sproul, R.C. *Chosen by God*. Carol Stream, IL: Tyndale, 2021. First printed in 1986. [A clear and forceful defense of the doctrine of election and the importance of that doctrine to our understanding of our salvation in Christ.]

Trueman, Carl R. *The Creedal Imperative*. Wheaton: Crossway, 2012. [This book makes the case that creeds and confessions are biblical and are necessary for the life of the church. It shows why confessions have been central in the past and why they must remain so in order for churches to remain healthy and sound.]

NOTES

Foreword

1 David E. Garland, *1 Corinthians*, Baker Exegetical Commentary on the New Testament (Grand Rapids: Baker Academic, 2003), 674.

Introduction: Theology Matters

1 Petrus Van Mastricht, *Theoretical-Practical Theology*, vol. 1, trans. Todd M. Rester (Grand Rapids: Reformation Heritage, 2018), 8.

Chapter 1: What Is Reformed Theology?

1 See, for example, Pss. 19:7–10; 119:89; John 10:35; 17:17; 2 Tim. 3:16.

2 The Catechism of the Catholic Church (paragraph 1367) states, "The sacrifice of Christ and the sacrifice of the Eucharist are *one single sacrifice*. . . . 'And since in this divine sacrifice which is celebrated in the Mass, the same Christ who offered himself once in a bloody manner on the altar of the cross is contained and is offered in an unbloody manner . . . this sacrifice is truly propitiatory.'" (Emphasis original.)

Chapter 2: Scripture and God's Sovereignty

1 Quoted in Michael A. G. Haykin, *The Revived Puritan: The Spirituality of George Whitefield* (Dundas, Ontario: Judson Press, 2000), 71–72.

Chapter 3: The Covenants

1 G. E. Mendenhall and G. A. Herion, "Covenant," in David Noel Freedman, ed., *Anchor Bible Dictionary* (New York: Doubleday, 1992), 1179.

2 Robert Rollock, "A Treatise of God's Effectual Calling" in *Select Works of Robert Rollock*, ed. William Gunn (Edinburgh: Woodrow Society, 1844), 31.

3 J. I. Packer, "Introduction: On Covenant Theology," in Herman Witsius, *The Economy of the Covenants between God and Man* (Grand Rapids: Reformation Heritage, 2010 reprint), 1:31–34.

Chapter 4: The Blessings of Reformed Theology

1 Westminster Confession of Faith, chapter 3.1.

2 John Calvin, *Institutes of the Christian Religion*, ed. John T. McNeill, trans. Ford Lewis Battles (Philadelphia: Westminster Press, 1960), 3.2.6.